PETER G. JOHNSON (ED.)

FLUVIAL PROCESSES

CUEILLETTE ET ANALYSE
DES DONNÉES

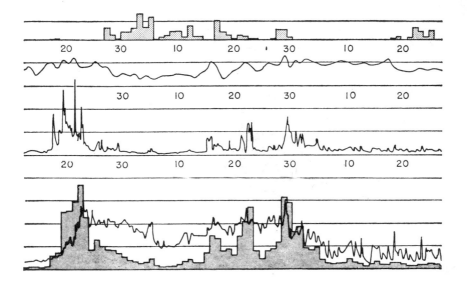

3

TRAVAUX DU
DÉPARTEMENT DE GÉOGRAPHIE
ET D'AMÉNAGEMENT RÉGIONAL
UNIVERSITÉ D'OTTAWA

OCCASIONAL PAPERS
DEPARTMENT OF GEOGRAPHY
AND REGIONAL PLANNING
UNIVERSITY OF OTTAWA

ÉDITIONS DE L'UNIVERSITÉ D'OTTAWA
UNIVERSITY OF OTTAWA PRESS
Ottawa, Canada
1975

FLUVIAL PROCESSES

CUEILLETTE ET ANALYSE
DES DONNÉES

Proceedings
the Third Annual Colloquium of the Department of Geography
and Regional Planning

March 24-25, 1972

Compte rendu
Troisième colloque du Département de Géographie et
d'Aménagement régional

24-25 mars 1972

© Éditions de l'Université d'Ottawa — University of Ottawa Press, 1975
ISBN-0-7766-3503-4

PETER G. JOHNSON (ED.)

FLUVIAL PROCESSES

CUEILLETTE ET ANALYSE
DES DONNÉES

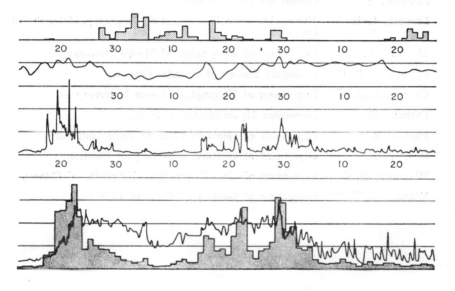

3

TRAVAUX DU
DÉPARTEMENT DE GÉOGRAPHIE
ET D'AMÉNAGEMENT RÉGIONAL
UNIVERSITÉ D'OTTAWA

OCCASIONAL PAPERS
DEPARTMENT OF GEOGRAPHY
AND REGIONAL PLANNING
UNIVERSITY OF OTTAWA

ÉDITIONS DE L'UNIVERSITÉ D'OTTAWA
UNIVERSITY OF OTTAWA PRESS
Ottawa, Canada
1975

COLLABORATEURS — CONTRIBUTORS

BROWN, M. C.   Department of Geography, University of Alberta.

CLÉMENT, P.   Département de Géographie, Université de Sherbrooke.

COGLEY, J. G.   Department of Geography, McMaster University.

DIONNE, J.-C.   Ministère Canadien de l'Environnement, Québec 10.

FORD, D.   Department of Geography, McMaster University.

LENGELLÉ, J.   Conseil des Arts, Ottawa.

LEOPOLD, L. B.   Visiting Professor, Department of Geography, University of Ottawa.

McCANN, S. B.   Department of Geography, McMaster University.

McDONALD, B. C.   Geological Survey of Canada, Ottawa.

ONGLEY, E. D.   Department of Geography, Queens University.

OSTREM, G.   Norwegian Hydro-Electricity Board.

PARKER, R. S.   Department of Geology, Colorado State University.

RUST, B. R.   Department of Geology, University of Ottawa.

WARNOCK, R. G.   Department of Civil Engineering, University of Ottawa.

WILKINSON, T. P.   Department of Geography, Carleton University.

PREFACE

The annual colloquium of the Department of Geography and Regional Planning has now become a well established meeting. Each year, a theme is proposed which is of current interest in the academic or applied aspects of the discipline. This collection of papers and abstracts is the result of the third colloquium, which was the first to consider a Geomorphological topic.

The Department was particularly grateful with respect to this colloquium to Dr. Luna B. Leopold (Visiting professor at the University of Ottawa) and to Dr. G. Østrem (Visiting professor at Carleton University).

The combining of the colloquium with the meeting of the Ontario Geomorphologists Group also helped to provide a forum for discussion between the Ontario and Quebec Geomorphologists as well as many other delegates.

AVANT-PROPOS

Le colloque annuel du Département de Géographie et d'Aménagement Régional est devenu un événement bien établi. Chaque année, le thème proposé est d'intérêt présent sur les aspects académiques ou appliqués de la discipline. Cette collection de documents est le résultat du troisième colloque qui considéra, pour la première fois, un sujet de géomorphologie.

Le Département est particulièrement reconnaissant, pour ce colloque, au Dr. Luna B. Leopold (professeur invité à l'Université d'Ottawa) et Dr. G. Østrem (professeur invité à l'Université de Carleton).

Le colloque, combiné à une réunion du groupe de géomorphologie de l'Ontario, a aussi favorisé de nombreuses discussions entre les géomorphologues du Québec et de l'Ontario ainsi que plusieurs autres délégués.

Dr. Denis A. St-Onge,
Chairman/Directeur.

ACKNOWLEDGEMENTS

The Department of Geography and Regional Planning wishes to thank the National Research Council of Canada for the financial assistance which contributed greatly to the success of the colloquium.

REMERCIEMENTS

Le Département de Géographie et d'Aménagement Régional désire remercier le Conseil National des Recherches du Canada pour l'assistance financière qui a permis à ce colloque d'être un succès.

TABLE DES MATIÈRES — TABLE OF CONTENTS

Plan and Depth Spectra of the Colorado River in Grand Canyon

M. C. BROWN,
Department of Geography,
University of Alberta

L. B. LEOPOLD,
Visiting Professor,
Department of Geography and Regional Planning,
University of Ottawa

Spectrum analysis is a way of disintegrating a complex wave-form into components. A common method involves calculation of the cross-covariance, and Fourier transformation from this into the variance spectrum. Assumptions involved are:

(1) the data are Gaussian or normally distributed.

(2) the data are stationary; that is, moving the origin will not change the spectrum.

Spectrum analysis consists of seeking, in a series of numbers, what distances apart in the series separate values that "correlate" with one another, whether the spacings are periodic or aperiodic. In the analysis discussed here, one set of data concerns values of depths of water at each 1/10th mile along the river length. The analysis consists of correlating the values of river depth at distances apart of 0.2, 0.3, 0.4, 0.5 miles, etc. It can be seen that the number of pieces of data available decreased as the spacing distance increases. If 1000 observations were available, there are only three values spaced at 33 miles. For spacing distance of 10 miles, how-ever, one would have a series consisting of miles 1.0, 11.0, 21.0, etc., and again 1.1, 11.1, 21.1, etc. Thus the number of values available for making the analysis increases rapidly as the spacing distance decreases.

Those distances apart that give the highest "correlation" there-fore are assumed to represent a repeating distance of depth, in this analysis, and reflect the effects of physical processes operating, such as the processes which form the repetitious pool and riffle sequence in small streams.

In the case of river data, it has been shown that small streams with pools and riffles have shallow spots spaced at 7 to 10 channel widths. The present problem is to determine whether similar repetitious patterns occur in an incised canyon river.

Spectrum analysis was first applied to the plan form of rivers by J. Ross Mackay in 1963, but J. Speight's work on the Angabunga was the first extensive use of the technique. The major advantage and purpose in using spectral techniques is that these obviate the need for subjective and arbitrary definition of meander wavelength, a quantity which is difficult to define for most rivers. Implicit in the use of spectral methods is the assumption that most rivers contain a range of meander wavelengths superimposed one on another. Speight found that the pattern of river directional changes (as in going around meander bends) had several repetitious distances or wave lengths, many more than the previously known distance of 7 to 10 river widths. The longer wavelengths are not obvious looking at a map and were discovered by application of spectrum analysis. Speight found that although the spectra for successive reaches of the Angabunga, and successive reaches over time, were stable, he could not relate the peaks to common functions of discharge. Chang and Toebes found instability in the spectra of sucessive downstream reaches, but this is not surprising because their data were very nonstationary.

Of great importance in spectrum calculations is the "balance" between "n" (number of data points) and "m" (number of lags for cross-covariance, and number of spectral line estimates).

Because increasing "m" gives a finer detailed spectrum, there is a temptation to have a n:m ratio of > 20%, but the significance (in a statistical sense) of the peaks does *not* increase; this is because the probability of noise peaks also increases. In general, about 10% seems to be desirable, but this is open to question.

Our data consisted of about 150 miles of river measured at 1/10*th* mile for depth of water at a constant discharge of 48,000 cfs and directional changes in plan view at the same points.

On initial examination of depth data for 4 reaches of the Colorado, after removing dimensions by dividing the wavelength peaks by over-all mean river widths, there appeared to be a good correlation between the Colorado depth peaks and the Angabunga *Note* plan peaks. These repetitive distances were:

6.0 — 6.6; 8.9 — 9.9; 15 — 17; 21 — 29; 58 — 59.

(t = 0.1 mile, n = 649, m = 65)

These values are the number of river widths representing repetition distances. The result is of interest because one river is very free to meander, the other not, but free to change its bed. It is emphasized that repetition distances were comparable in data on meanders, and for the Colorado bed changes.

We then considered meander spectra of the Colorado. At first, for all reaches, this was discouraging. Not only were the (dimensionless) meander peaks apparently not related to the Angabunga meander peaks (which we would have predicted), but they were apparently not even related to the Colorado depth peaks. But when we overlaid the actual spectra of the two Colorado series, there appeared a strong *inverse* correlation between plan and depth spectra. For the longest reach, 46.1 — 110.8, the inverse correlation is striking and highly significant. We postulate that this implies something about river behaviour as a whole. A peak in the spectrum indicates a greater than expected contribution to the total variance of the system — the area under the spectrum is the whole series variance. Thus a single peak would indicate one meander frequency. The inverseness shows that *if*, at a given frequency, a *greater* than average contribution to the total variance is found in the meander spectrum, then, for the same frequency, a *less* than average contribution to the total variance will be made by the depth variance spectrum. We conclude:

1. The river operates to smooth the sum of its plan and depth spectra; i.e., there is a *complimentary* relation between the spectra.

2. Although it has been known for a long time that rivers dissipate energy by bed form configurations in the small scale, and recently established that they smooth their energy grade line by dissipating energy by meanders, this complimentarity strongly suggests:

a. that bed forms which dissipate energy operate on a far larger scale than previously imagined.

b. that meanders and depth changes together, in three dimensions, act to smooth the energy grade line, and thereby
distribute work efficiently.

At several wavelengths the inverseness breaks down and both
bed form and plan form spectra show peaks: at these frequencies
(dimensionless 4.7, 6.4, 10.6, 25.8) the river seems to resonate in
three dimensions. The cross spectral statistic (coherence)[2], an exact
analogue in the frequency domain of the correlation coefficient
(more properly coefficient of determination) r^2, supports this, and
has peaks significant at between 5 and 10% at these frequencies.

Now the relation with the Angabunga seems more understand-
able. We think that the Angabunga meanders and Colorado bedforms are similar in dimensionless terms. We surmise that the Angabunga bedforms inversely correlate with the Colorado meanders.
Further, we predict that the dimensionless (meanders on the Angabunga, bedforms on the Colorado) series will be found in the
meanders of all rivers free to meander in unconsolidated materials,
and in the bedforms of all other rivers.

A preliminary investigation of the *depth* spectra of the N. Saskatchewan River, downstream from Edmonton (n = 500, m = 50,
t = 0.1 mile), shows that for this confined river, dimensionless peaks
occur at 25.6 and 54.5. We regard this as tentative support of the
above hypotheses, and thank the Alberta Research Council for allow-
ing us access to unpublished data.

Sediment Transport Studies at Selected Glacier Streams in Norway 1969

Dr. G. Østrem,
Norwegian Hydro-Electricity Board

English Summary from "Slamtransportundersökelser i Norske Bre-Elver 1969".
Rapport NR 6/70, Vassdragsdirektoratet Hydrologisk Avdeling, Oslo, Sept. 1970.

INTRODUCTION

The sediment transport studies presently being undertaken at Norwegian glacier streams is a joint venture between the Norwegian Water Resources and Electricity Board and the Department of Physical Geography at Stockholm University. The aim of the investigations is to gain knowledge about the magnitudes and variations of sediment transport in glacier streams including the study of deposition of such material. The obtained data has an important bearing on the planning of the future hydro-electric projects utilizing glacier meltwater streams and also for studying glacier erosion which the transported sediments are a result of.

The map (Fig. 1) shows the distribution of observation stations. There is a wide range of variation in the climatic, geological and glaciological conditions between the selected glaciers.

At each observation station a small hut for two observers has been erected and the stations are usually manned for 3-4 months during the summer. From these stations water samples are collected close to the glacier fronts and in some cases at sites further downstream as well. Meteorological, glaciological and water discharge observations are also carried out at the glaciers.

The main effort of the present studies has been devoted to the transport of suspended material. Some attention has also been given to the accumulation of coarse material in river deltas. In 1969 it was attempted to determine the bed load transport from Nigardsbreen by trapping all the coarse material in a constructed steel-net. A description of this experiment is given in the present volume.

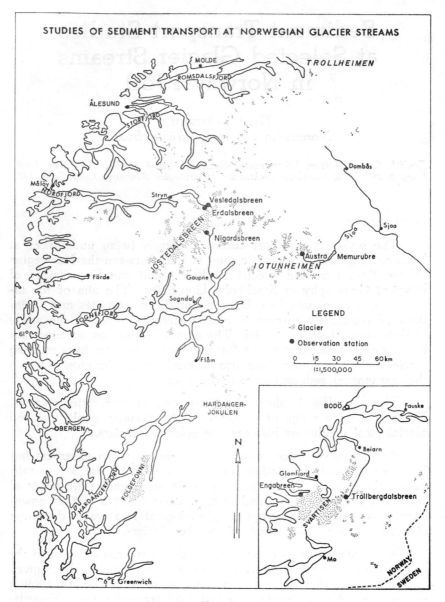

Fig. 1.

METHODS

Water samples are generally collected 2-5 times daily at one or more observation sites along the selected glacier streams during a field period. During flood conditions samples are taken hourly. The samples are collected in 1-litre plastic bottles and then filtered. After filtration in the field the filter papers with sediment particles are sent to the laboratory for ashing before the content of suspended sediment in the samples is determined. Water discharge is calculated from water-level records or from frequent visual staff-gauge readings.

The volumes of sediment transport at a given watercourse are computed on the basis of measured sediment concentrations from the samples, coupled with discharge figures. (For further description of the computations, see below).

SOURCES OF ERRORS

The method of sampling probably gives rise to the main source of error in the determination of sediment transport volumes. It is not clear to what extent one sample should be regarded as typical for the whole river profile at the sampling site, and further, whether it is representative for a certain time period. An investigation into this problem will be carried out in 1970.

The fact that the field period does not cover the entire sediment transport season introduces a further complication. The apparent unpredictability of the volume of sediment transport in relation to discharge through the year makes estimations of such transport unreliable, especially as there seems to be a frequent occurrence of one or several high peaks of water discharge after the annual field period has terminated. It is therefore intended to extend the observation period in the late part of the summer.

Finally, there is the problem of calculating the volume of water discharge passing sampling sites where reliable gauging is difficult. This is the case at three of the five selected water courses. At these three there exist natural sedimentation basins (a lake) a short distance below the glacier front and sampling is done both at the inlets and outlets of the lakes to study their trap efficiency. Since the installed water gauges record discharge *from* the lakes only, the amount of water draining from the glacier *into* the lakes must be calculated. A model for such calculation has been developed incorporating observed variations in water storage in the lakes and

figures for precipitation that adds water to the system between the
two sampling sites (see Fig. 3). Since determination of discharge
into the lakes is based on an indirect method of computation this
must be regarded as a possible source of errors.

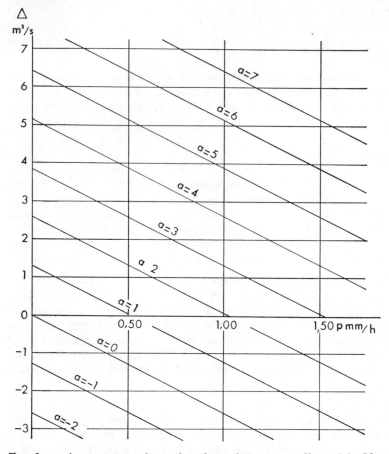

Fig. 3. — the nomogram shows the relation between runoff into lake Nigardsvatn,
discharge from the lake, rising or falling water level and precipitation.
Example: Increasing water level 2 cms/h (a = +2) precipitation
12mm per day (p = 0.5). The intersection between the lines a = +2
and p = 0.5 gives the value ▲ = 1.4 m³/s, which means that water
into the lake is 1.4 m³s higher than out of the lake.

DATA PROCESSING

The calculations involved to determine volumes of sediment transport are very time-consuming, and with the recent extension in the number of observed glaciers it has been necessary to develop a computer programme to cope with the data.

The programme is designed to handle observations from single sampling sites as well as data from the inlets and outlets of the sedimentation basins in combination, for determination of their trap efficiency. In the latter case the computer calculates the discharge into the lake by modifying the observed discharge of the outlet, taking into account variations in water storage of the lake together with precipitation in the drainage area between the inlet and outlet (mentioned above).

The water discharge at each sampling site is computed for every hour of the day. In cases where continuous water records are not available hourly values for water stage are generated by the computer through linear interpolation between existing observations. Hourly sediment concentrations are obtained similarly by linear interpolation between the known concentrations of collected samples. The volume of hourly sediment transport is then computed by multiplication of water discharge and sediment concentration for the same hour.

The computer outprint gives hourly values for water stage, water discharge into the lake and out of the lake, sediment concentration and sediment transport (metric tons per hour) into and out of the lake. Finally, the total daily water discharge and sediment transport at the sampling sites are printed.

THE "FENCE" PROJECT AT NIGARDSBREEN,
A STUDY OF BED LOAD TRANSPORT

The river draining from Nigardsbreen transports considerable amounts of coarse material. During days of high water discharge the movement of large rocks along the river bed can be indirectly observed by a particularly strong and irregular noise caused by boulders striking each other. (At the entrance to Nigardsvatn a delta is formed by the gradual accumulation of the bulky material at the inlet of the lake.) Routine measurements of increment in the delta volume are described below.

In 1969 an attempt was made to measure the bed load transport in the river draining from the front of Nigardsbreen by means of a

steel net erected across the river. The net was erected at a site
where the river passes over exposed bedrock in a relatively broad
and flat channel. It was constructed as a fence, consisting of 4 mm
steel wires with mesh size 2 x 6 cm, 50 m wide and 2.5 m high
and it was supported by a steel construction drilled into the bedrock, held in position by heavy steel cables. A coordinate system
was erected on the upstream side of the net to measure the rate
of agglomeration. The surface of the accumulating material was
surveyed regularly along fixed cross-sections by levelling. The total
number of measuring points was 180, covering an area of 720 m².
The total accumulation from May 24th, when the net was erected,
till the end of June (when it broke due to an unusually high flood)
amounted to approx. 400 metric tons of coarse material. Within
the same period approx. 1,270 metric tons of suspended material
passed the sampling site at the net. The ratio of bed load to
suspended material, based on measurements from the period, was
approx. 1:3. However, the mesh size allowed a certain portion of
the sand and gravel fractions in the bed load to penetrate the net.
Hence, it is likely that the quoted figure, 400 tons, should be increased somewhat to give the true volume of the bed load transport.
The relation between bed load and suspended material moved by
stream in this period was therefore at least 1:3, probably much
higher.

STUDIES OF SEDIMENT TRANSPORT, DEPOSITION AND DELTA DEVELOP-
MENT IN NATURAL SEDIMENTATION BASINS

At the three glaciers with the previously mentioned natural
sedimentation basins, sediment sampling was performed both at the
lake entrances and at the outlets. In addition studies of delta formation were performed at Nigardsvatn and Vesledalsvatn.

NIGARDSBREEN

For Nigardsbreen it was found that 13,910 metric tons of fine
material was discharged into the lake during the observation period
(94 days). During the same time interval 3,440 tons were carried
out of the lake. Approx. 10,000 tons were thus deposited on the
lake bottom, while the total water discharge was measured to 183
million m³. The corresponding figures for 1968 (see Tornas, 1969)
were 4,370 tons of sediment into the lake and 1,375 out of the lake.
For 1962 Wehn states that 2,530 tons went into the lake and 728

left the lake (Wehn, 1965, p. 60). However, the 1962 values were obtained when the glacier front was still situated in the lake itself so that the samples could not be taken in a well-defined melt water river. These values are therefore probably too small.

The measurements of the accumulation in the delta at lake Nigardsvatn are carried out by a combination of levelling and depth sounding at altogether 290 single points. The points are located along fixed cross sections. Measurements are repeated at the same points every year and the accuracy of measurement in the vertical on a level surface is ± 0.5 cm (on steep slopes up to a couple of centimeters either way). From the measurements it is calculated that approx. 9,500 tons of material were deposited in the delta area west of the cross-section between pts. 14 and 15 (see Fig. 12) during one year which gives an average accumulation of 16.9 cm over the surface of that area. Coarse material constitutes a high percentage of this amount. A rough comparison with the volume of silt transported from the glacier in the field period 1969 indicates that the bed load transport may have formed a larger proportion of the total transported volume than the net project showed. On the basis of the accumulation measurements it is therefore likely, that bed load transport can make up as much as 50% of the total transport of material from Nigardsbreen.

VESLEDALSBREEN

At Vesledalsbreen sediment samples were collected at three sampling sites: (A) in the stream near the glacier front, (B) approx.

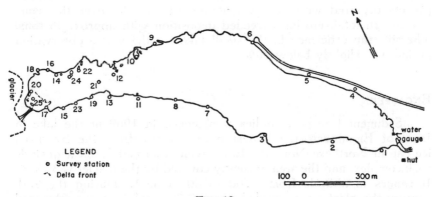

Fig. 12.

1 km downstream from the front, at the entrance to lake Vesledal-svatn (surface area 1,800 m²) and (C), at the outlet of the lake (see Fig. 15). In addition, accumulation measurements were carried out by depth soundings in the small lake in a similar way to that at Nigardsvatn.

The observed results of the sediment transport, discharge and meteorological measurements from Vesledalsbreen 1969 are shown in the diagrams in Fig. 16. For the field period June 12 — August 29, calculations of discharge based on staff-gauge readings at sampling site A together with the known concentrations of sediment samples, show that the volume of silt transported in the stream at the glacier front was 579 metric tons.

Further, it is calculated that 617 metric tons of suspended material entered the lake while 328 metric tons were carried out of the lake: approx. 290 tons must thus have been deposited on the lake bottom.

Five cross-sections constituting a total of 90 single sounding points were measured in Vesledalsvatn to determine the accumulation in the lake since the measurement in 1968 (see Fig. 14). It was found that the accumulation of material in the lake amounted to approx. 1,590 metric tons. This figure must be regarded as unusually high and should be treated with caution till it is verified by measurements next year.

The table in Fig. 17 shows a subdivision of the total field period into 8 shorter periods. During four of these periods it can be seen that an erosion occured along the river bed between sampling stations A and B while during the remaining periods the reverse process occurred with an accumulation of material over the same stretch. In total, erosion exceeded deposition with approx. 38 tons. The silt trap efficiency in the small lake for the whole observation period was slightly below 50%.

ENGABREEN

Sediment transport studies commenced in 1969 at the lake in front of Engabreen, the largest outlet glacier from the Svartisen ice-cap in Northern Norway. Engabreen rests mainly on a gneissic rock complex, and the area presently covered by the glacier is 39 km². It ranges in altitude from 1,600 to 80 m a.s.l. During the 20th century the glacier has receded approx. 2km, while it has advanced

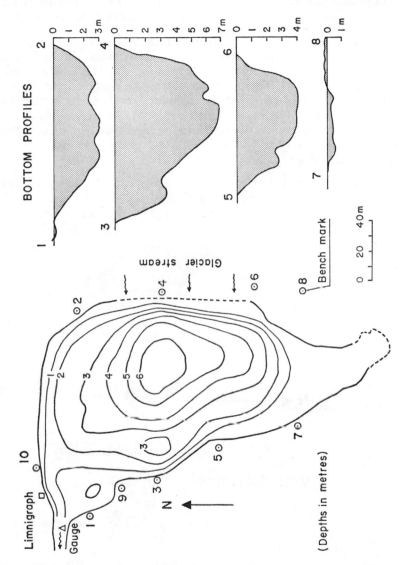

Fig. 14. — Map and sounding profiles for accumulation measurements, Vesledalsvatn. On the map the location of bench marks and the sites of the staff gauge and water-level recorder (Limnigraph) are plotted.

slightly again in the last few years. The area of the lake is 1.2 km²,
its maximum depth is 90 m and the lake surface lies 10 m a.s.1.

Fig. 20 shows the results of the 1969 observations of discharge,
sediment transport and meteorological parameters. The sediment concentrations of the meltwater discharging into the lake ranged from
20-350 mg/1. At the outlet concentrations ranged from 4-70 mg/1.
During the field period it is calculated that 8,650 metric tons of
suspended material were carried out of it. Hence, approx. 77% of
the suspended material carried into the lake sedimented there between
June 23 — August 18. In the same period the water discharge
was 103. 10^6m³ water.

It is estimated that the total transport of suspended material
from Engabreen during 1969 was 9,500 metric tons. Bed load
measurements have not been carried out. The experience from

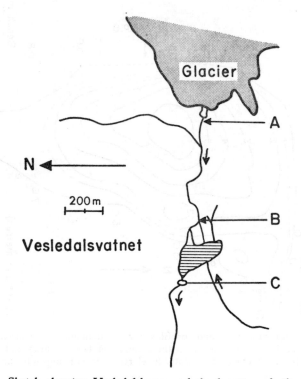

Fig. 15. — Sketch showing Vesledalsbreen and the location of silt-sampling stations in the watercourse draining from the glacier.

	1967	1968	1969
A. Suspended Material	630	303	579 tons
Discharge			17.21 - 10⁶m³
Accumulation along the river		−191	−38 tons
B. Suspended Material		494	617 tons
Accumulation in lake			
a) Suspended Material	140	103	235 tons
b) Bed Load			1590 tons
C. Suspended Material		391	382 tons
Discharge		11.0 - 10⁶	20.54 - 10⁶m³
Precipitation			235mm

Fig. 17. — Synopsis of observations for 1969, 1968 and 1967 from Vesledalsbreen.

Nigardsbreen makes it reasonable to estimate that bed load transport from Engabreen constitutes approx. 30% of the volume of transported suspended material. Thus, the probable total transported volume of eroded material from Engabreen in 1969 would amount to approx. 12,500 metric tons. This volume corresponds to an erosion of approx. 0.16 mm evenly distributed over the bedrock surface under Engabreen.

ERDALSBREEN

The sediment transport studies initiated at Erdalsbreen in 1967 were continued in 1969. Erdalsbreen rests on a gneissic rock complex and is an outlet glacier on the western side of the Jostedalsbreen ice-cap and is the southern neighbour of Vesledalsbreen with an area of 11 km² and an altitudinal range 1,800 — 870 m a.s.1. The glacier front has retreated considerably during the 20th century. The

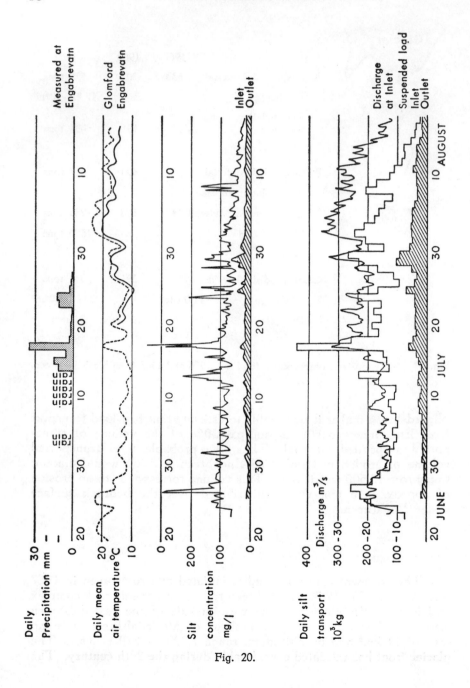

Fig. 20.

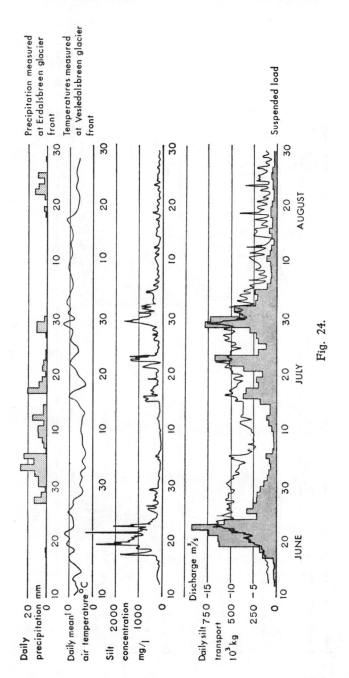

Fig. 24.

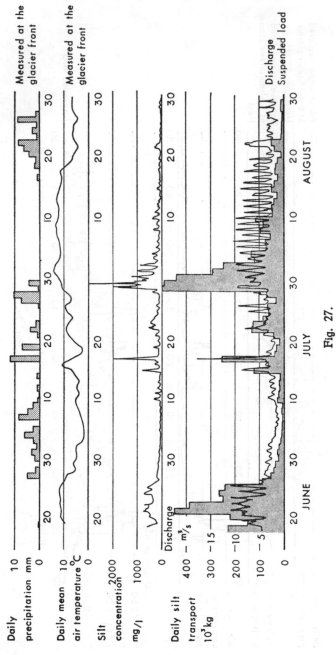

Fig. 27.

lower part of the glacier is surrounded by steep mountain sides and the glacier is fed through tributary icefalls along the sides.

The field period lasted from June 13 till August 29. Results of sediment transport, discharge and meteorological observations are shown in the diagrams in Fig. 24. The sediment concentrations in the samples from the Erdalsbreen glacier stream ranged from 15 — 3,290 mg/1. It is estimated that approx. $\frac{1}{4}$ of the total transport during the field period occurred during five consecutive days at the beginning of the summer from June 19 — June 23. Within the total field period approx. 14,729 metric tons of suspended material were transported by the stream from the glacier front. In the same period $44.10^6 m^3$ of water was discharged from the glacier. It is estimated that a total of some 16,000 tons of suspended material was transported from Erdalsbreen during the melt season in 1969. If the bed load transport is taken to be 30% of the load in suspension, the total transport of material from Erdalsbreen in 1969 will be of the order of 25,000 tons. Evenly distributed on the glacier bed this corresponds to at least 0.95 mm of erosion under the glacier, which is 3-4 times as much as observed at the other glaciers in Southern Norway.

Austre Memurubre

Studies of sediment transport at Austre Memurubre were continued in 1969. Austre Memurubre is a cirque-glacier situated in Jotunheimen. The glacier is surrounded by high mountain sides and rests on basic plutonic rock (Jotun-noritt). The glacier area is 9 km² and the altitudinal range 2,250 — 1,690 m a.s.1. Movement studies carried out in 1968/69 showed that the glacier moves slowly, 8 metres p.a. in the centre and less than 1 metre p.a. at the tongue.

In the 20th century the glacier front has receded approx. 1 km and in the newly exposed area a considerable layer of loose and easily erodible glacial deposits remain. Approx. 10 smaller streams issuing from the glacier front drain through this area. 1.5 km downstream from the front all the streams unite in one watercourse. Here a recording stage gauge has been set up and water samples are collected at this site.

The observed values of the sediment transport, discharge and meteorological observations from Austre Memurubre 1969 are shown diagrammatically in (see Fig. 27). The sediment concentrations of samples taken in the river varied between 11 mg/1 — 3,037 mg/1.

It is calculated that approx. 6,880 metric tons of suspended material were carried by the river at the sampling site during the field period 1969. While approx. $26.10^6 m^3$ of water was discharged past the site during this time.

It is obvious that not all of the transported material has originated from beneath the glacier; several very heavy rainstorms occured during the field period eroding the area of glacial deposits in front of the glacier. Erosion along the stream beds was also observed. It is estimated, therefore, that only some 4,500 metric tons of the measured sediment transport originated exclusively from the glacierized area, while the total transport of material passing the front of Austre Memurubre in 1969, bed load included, was probably of the order of 6,500 metric tons. This is equivalent to 0.26 mm erosion evenly distributed over the whole bedrock surface under Austre Memurubre.

CONCLUSION

A synopsis of the results from the investigations in 1969 are presented in the table in Fig. 29 together with the results of studies from previous years. The table demonstrates clearly the variations in the volumes of transported sediments that exist between the individual glaciers which were investigated. Further, fluctuations in the volumes of transport for one and the same glacier from year to year are revealed. Continued studies will aim at clarifying those factors that may help to understand these variations. The reliability of the sampling method must be investigated together with possible alternative methods. The field periods must be extended to cover the whole season of high water discharge. Further studies of bed load transport are desirable. Over a longer period it seems that studies of delta formation will yield good results at low cost. The presence of natural sedimentation basins just in front of many Norwegian glaciers facilitates well-distributed studies of this kind.

At the studied glacier streams samples are collected close to the glacier fronts (except Memurubreen), and it must be assumed that the measured quantities of sediment are a product of glacial erosion. However, the amount of material transported annually by the glacier stream will not necessarily reflect the annual erosion caused by the glacier. Certain parts of the material produced during one single year may be stored under the glacier and flushed out by a peak in the melt water discharge next year or later. Some of the material may have been produced when the glaciers were

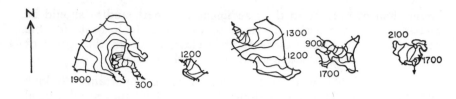

Glacier Name	Nigards- breen	Vesledals- breen	Enga- breen	Erdals- breen	Austre Memurubre
Area Km²	40	4	39	11	9
No. of weeks with observations		7		6	9
Observed silt transport. tons.		530		7840	4700
Estimated total annual transport.		1000		15000	6000
Sediment Yield, tons/km²		250		1360	630
Corresponding erosion in mm.		0.12		0.70	0.22
No. of weeks with observations	12	11		10	11
Observed silt transport. tons.	4370	300		6300	3300
Estimated total annual transport.	6000	500		10000	4500
Sediment yield, tons/km²	150	125		910	500
Corresponding erosion in mm.	0.07	0.06		0.45	0.18
No. of weeks with observations	13	11	8	11	10
Observed silt transport. tons.	13910	579	8650	14720	6880
Estimated total annual transport.	22000	900	12500	21000	6500
Sediment yield tons/km²	550	225	320	1910	720
Corresponding erosion in mm.	0.27	0.11	0.16	0.95	0.26

Fig. 29. — Investigations of sediment yield at selected glaciers in Norway.

larger than at present so that, sediment transport studies should be carried out over a series of years to form a reliable basis for the determination of glacier erosion. It is clear, however, that some of the studied glaciers produce more material than others.

As stated above, it is a matter of some importance to look into the causes of these variations. Some further studies, additional to those already accomplished, should yield valuable results. The magnitude of glacial erosion depends on the geological and topographical characteristics of the rock subjected to erosion and the volume and rate of movement of the eroding agent. Investigations of the geology at the studied glaciers coupled with a volumetric survey by radioecho techniques and an extension of the present movement studies are therefore desirable. In conjunction with this, mineral analysis of the transported material would be valuable. A concentration of the efforts outlined above coupled with the existing glaciological, meteorological and hydrological sediment transport studies already in existence should yield further results of both practical and scientific value.

BIBLIOGRAPHY

AHLBERT, I. B., og SJÖBERG, B., (1962), "Nagra metodiska undersökningar för beräkning av slamtransporten i Tarfalajokk", *Prosem. uppsats*, 1962, Naturgeogr. Inst., Stockholms Universitet, 17 p.

BAGNOLD, R. A., (1954), "Some flume experiments on large grains but little denser than the transporting fluid, and their implications", Inst. Civil Engrs. Proc. Paper No. 6041, p. 174-205.

BERGERSEN, A., (1953), "En undersökelse av Svartisen ved Holandsfjorden 1950-1951", Hovedfagsoppgave ved Georg. Inst., Universitetet i Oslo (upublisert), 55 p. + ill.

CÉWE, T., og NORRBIN, J., (1965), "Tarfalajakk, Ladtjojakka och Ladtjojaure. Vattenföring, slamtransport och sedimentation", *Ymer*, 1965, p. 85-111.

EKMAN, S. R., (1969), "Nigardsvatnet som sedimentationsbassäng", in PYTTE, R. (ed.), *Glasiologiske Undersökelser i Norge*, 1968, (149 p.). Rapport nr. 5/69, Vassdragsdirektoratet, Hydrologisk avdeling, p. 123-133, (with an English summary).

ELG, M., og GUSTAVSSON, L., (1970), "Detaljstudier av vattenföringens och slamtransportens vertikala variation längs med en känd bäckfara", *Prosem. uppsats*, 1970, Naturgeogr. Inst., Stockholms Universitet, 15 p.

HOLTEDAHL, O., (1960), "Engabreen area", in HOLTEDAHL, Föyn og Reitan, *Aspects of the Geology of Northern Norway* (66 p.). Guide to excursion no. A 3, Norges Geologiske Undersökelse No. 212 a, p. 17-25.

HUBBELL, D. W., (1963), "Apparatus and techniques for measuring bed load", U.S. Geol. Survey Water Supply Paper No. 1748, 74 p.

LEOPOLD, L. B., WOHLMAN, M. G., og MILLER, J. P., (1964), Fluvial Processes in Geomorphology, p. 151-197.

LIESTÖL, O., (1962), "Special investigations on Hellstugubreen and Tverrabreen", in HOEL and WERENSKJOLD, Glaciers and Snowfields in Norway, Norsk Polarinstitutt, Skrifter Nr. 114, 219 p., p. 175-207.

LUNDQVIST, G., (1937), "Recenta isavsmältningar och finmaterialets transport", Norsk Geogr. Tidskrift, Vol. VI (1936-37), p. 15-24.

NIELSEN, Chr., (1970), "Trianguleringer og bevegelsesberegninger 1969", in PYTTE, R. (ed.), Glasiologiske undersökelser i Norge 1969 (96 p.), Rapport no. 5/70, Vassdragsdirektoratet, Hydrologisk avdeling, p. 60-71.

PYTTE, R., (1970), "Materialhusholdningen og meteorologiske og hydrologiske undersökelser ved utvalgte breer", in PYTTE, R. (ed.), Glasiologiske undersökelser i Norge 1969 (96 p.). Rapport no. 5/70, Vassdragsdirektoratet, Hydrologisk avdeling, p. 4-60.

REKSTAD, I., (1912), "Die Ausfüllung eines Sees vor dem Engabrä, dem grössten Ausläufer des Svartisen, als Mass der Gletschererosion", Zeitschrift für Gletscherkunde, Vol. VI, p. 212-214.

RICHTER, K., (1936), "Gefügestudien im Engabre, Fondalsbre und ihren Vorlandsedimenten", Zeitschrift für Gletscherkunde, Vol. XXIV, p. 22-30.

TORNAS, S., (1968), "Slamtransport i noen utvalgte bre-elver", in ØSTREM og PYTTE (ed.), Glasiologiske undersökelser i Norge 1967 (131 p.), Rapport no. 4/68, Vassdragsdirektoratet, Hydrologisk avdeling, p. 67-69.

— (1969), "Slamtransport i noen utvalgte bre-elver", in PYTTE, R. (ed.), Glasiologiske undersökelser i Norge 1968, 149 p., Rapport no. 5/69, Vassdragsdirektoratet, p. 97-123.

WEHN, D., (1965), "Vannförings-og slamundersökelser i Nigardsbreens vassdrag", Hovedfagsoppgave ved Geogr. Inst., Universitetet i Oslo (upublisert), 94 p.

ØSTREM, G., (1969), "Korrelasjonsberegninger og regresjonsanalyser av dögnlig avlöp som funksjon av meteorologiske parametre", in PYTTE, R. (ed.), Glasiologiske undersökelser i Norge 1968 (149 p.), Rapport no. 5/69, Vassdragsdirektoratet, Hydrologisk avdeling, p. 83-97.

ØSTREM, G., og STANLEY, A., Glacier Mass Balance Measurements. A Manual for Field and Office Work, Canadian Dept. of Energy, Mines and Resources and Norw. Water Res. and Electricity Board, 125 p.

L'action morpho-sédimentologique des glaces dans le Saint-Laurent estuarien

J.-C. Dionne,
Ministère canadien de l'Environnement, Québec

RÉSUMÉ

Avec les vagues et les courants, les glaces constituent l'un des principaux agents morpho-sédimentologiques du Saint-Laurent. Huit années d'observations ont permis de dresser un bilan adéquat du rôle complexe des glaces dans un fleuve à marée. Les glaces sont à la fois un agent d'érosion, de transport, de sédimentation et de protection. Leur action morpho-sédimentologique se révèle trés variée et demeure encore mal connue ou sous-estimée de la plupart des spécialistes. Chaque année, les glaces prélèvent et transportent des millions de tonnes de sédiments. Elles érodent les rivages et y abandonnent une charge de matériel détritique considérable.

L'exposé permettra de voir par l'image l'action géologique des glaces dans la prise en charge, le transport, l'érosion et la sédimentation dans les principaux milieux intertidaux: bas estran, slikke, schorre, et de constater la nécessité d'étudier le rôle actif de cet agent dans le façonnement des rivages du Saint-Laurent. Les applications pratiques seront soulignées à l'occasion.

L'action morpho-sédimentologique des glaces flottantes se révèle assez complexe et variée suivant les milieux dans lesquels elle s'exerce. D'une façon générale cette action se manifeste sous quatre aspects principaux intimement liés les uns aux autres: érosion, transport, sédimentation et protection.

1. — ÉROSION

L'érosion par les glaces flottantes doit être considérée sous deux chefs principaux: l'érosion des roches consolidées et l'érosion des roches meubles.

a) Sur les roches consolidées, l'érosion ou l'abrasion glacielle directe peut être considérée minime. Sur les roches dures et non altérées, elle est pratiquement nulle; mais sur les roches tendres ou altérées, elle est facilement perceptible et semble parfois suffisamment importante pour être prise en considération dans l'étude des processus de destruction des littoraux. En effet, les glaces flottantes, armées ou non d'outils abrasifs, sont capables de polir, d'égratigner, de strier et de rainurer les roches tendres: calcaires, schistes argileux, grès, etc. Il existe de nombreuses observations à ce sujet (DIONNE, 1972c). Elles sont capables aussi d'affouiller et de raboter les plates-formes rocheuses littorales dont la surface est déjà altérée.

Indépendamment de la dureté relative de la roche, les glaces exercent en outre une action érosive indirecte sur les côtes rocheuses soit en délogeant des fragments déjà délimités par des diaclases, soit en favorisant la cryoclastie et en évacuant le matériel.

b) L'action érosive des glaces flottantes se manifeste principalement dans les roches meubles, en particulier sur les côtes affectées par des marées de moyenne à forte amplitude. D'une part les glaces érodent le fond en y creusant des rainures et des dépressions diverses, de l'autre, en prélevant une quantité déterminée de matériel meuble qu'elles déplacent sur des distances plus ou moins grandes. Cette action s'observe dans les différents milieux de sédimentation et dans diverses zones:

— sur les plages, on observe des rainures superficielles, des cicatrices d'arrachement et de poussée glacielle (HUME & SCHALK, 1964; DIONNE, 1968b, 1970);

— sur les bas estrans, on note des rainures linéaires et des mares d'affouillement (BROCHU, 1961; CAILLEUX & HAMELIN, 1967; ZENKOVICH, 1967; DIONNE, 1968c, 1969);

— dans les slikkes vaseuses ou sableuses, les rainures linéaires, les cuvettes d'affouillement et d'arrachement sont multiples (TARR, 1897; REINECK, 1956; DIONNE, 1969b, 1971a);

— dans les schorres ou les marais, on observe principalement des mares d'arrachement, des déchirures et des bouleversements divers et un fauchage systématique du tapis végétal (DIONNE, 1968a, 1972a);

— dans les zones plus profondes (fond de lacs et plates-formes prélittorales), on connaît plusieurs exemples de rainures linéaires (STANLEY, 1955; KOSHECHKIN, 1958; WEBER, 1958; PELLETIER & SHEARER, 1972).

2. — TRANSPORT

Le transport de matériel détritique et organique par les glaces flottantes est connu depuis fort longtemps. En effet, les glaces déplacent chaque année sur les côtes du monde plusieurs millions de tonnes de sédiments allant de la taille des colloïdes à celle des blocs de quelques mètres de diamètre. Cette action conditionne la sédimentation et une partie de l'érosion. Elle sert en quelque sorte de trait d'union entre l'action négative (érosion) et l'action positive (sédimentation) des glaces flottantes.

Le transport s'effectue selon trois modalités principales qui découlent du mode de prise en charge.

a) Le matériel peut être transporté alors qu'il est soudé à la base des glaçons ou des radeaux de glace. Dans ce cas, les distances parcourues sont relativement courtes, voire de l'ordre du kilomètre, car dès que les glaces viennent en contact avec des eaux plus chaudes, la "matrice" fond et laisse tomber le matériel détritique sur le fond.

b) Il peut aussi être transporté à la surface des glaçons ou des radeaux de glace. Dans ce cas, les distances franchies sont plus importantes, voire de l'ordre de la dizaine de kilomètres; mais à la condition que la mer ne soit pas trop agitée, car autrement, le matériel détritique à la surface des glaçons est lessivé et entraîné au fond rapidement, ou encore les glaçons chavirent et le matériel au contact de l'eau se détache et est disséminé progressivement au rythme de la fonte.

c) Il peut aussi être transporté incorporé à la glace. Dans ce cas, les distances franchies peuvent atteindre la centaine de kilomètres suivant le trajet suivi par les glaces de dérive et le temps requis pour la fonte.

La charge détritique transportée par les glaces flottantes peut théoriquement équivaloir au dixième de leur volume et parfois davantage puisque les glaces littorales (qui sont les plus souvent chargées de matériaux détritiques), sont fréquemment composées de blocs agglomérés et de glace non parfaitement cristallisée dont la densité est inférieure à celle de la glace pure.

Plusieurs estimations ont été faites sur la charge détritique des glaces flottantes. BROCHU (1961) évalue entre 0,5 et 1 kg la charge de sédiments d'un glaçon d'un mètre carré. BANCROFT (1905) estime à 72.000 tonnes au mille carré la charge en sédiments des glaçons du bassin de Minas (baie de Fundy). MILLER (1966) évalue à 198 grammes par pied cube de glace la charge en sédiments fins dans la baie de Fundy. HIND (1895) a calculé qu'une seule banquise dans l'estuaire de l'Avon (Nouvelle-Écosse), transportait 93.750 tonnes de vases. CRARY (1956) mentionne qu'une couche de limon éolien à la surface d'une île de glace dans l'Arctique contenait 120 grammes par mètre carré, alors que CAMPBELL et COLLINS (1958) estiment que dans le bassin de Fox, la teneur en sédiments fins atteint entre 0,05 et 2 grammes par kilo de glace; ce qui représente entre 4 et 8 millions de tonnes de sédiments transportés annuellement dans ce secteur arctique. Enfin BIRD (1967) estime qu'à South Bay (île de Southampton), en juin 1950, les débris à la surface de la glace totalisaient environ 10 tonnes à l'acre.

Pour le moyen estuaire du Saint-Laurent, nous avons estimé à plusieurs milliers de tonnes les sédiments transportés annuellement par les glaces flottantes (DIONNE, 1969b, 1971).

Ces quelques estimations permettent une évaluation approximative du rôle des glaces flottantes dans le transport de sédiments dans les régions froides. Il conviendrait donc de nuancer quelque peu le concept communément admis par la majorité des géologues à l'effet que les glaces flottantes représentent un agent de transport particulier guère plus important que les agents biologiques (algues, radeaux de végétation, troncs d'arbres, animaux, etc.).

Bien qu'en réalité il n'y ait pas de prise en charge *sensu stricto,* il convient de mentionner aussi les déplacements de sédiments dus aux glaces flottantes. En effet, le matériel poussé par les glaces s'inscrit dans les processus de transport.

3. — SÉDIMENTATION

Par son caractère positif, la sédimentation glacielle constitue probablement l'action la plus significative des glaces flottantes, car elle peut être reconnue aussi bien dans les formations anciennes que dans les formations récentes.

Par les quantités substantielles de matériel apportées dans les zones littorales et prélittorales, sur les plates-formes continentales et même dans les bassins profonds des régions froides, la sédimentation glacielle s'avère un phénomène d'une importance jusqu'à maintenant mal évaluée. Pourtant la plupart des chercheurs qui ont étudié la sédimentation des bassins arctiques ont reconnu sans équivoque qu'une grande partie du matériel (parfois plus de 50%) des zones prélittorales avait été apportée par les glaces flottantes (GRANT, 1956; PELLETIER, 1969).

Les apports glaciels ont pour conséquence une perturbation des conditions normales de sédimentation; ce qui se traduit par un faciès distinctif, caractérisé par une grande hétérométrie granulométrique, morphoscopique et minéralogique du matériel (TRASK, 1932; DIONNE, 1968b).

L'action sédimentologique des glaces flottantes s'exerce à la fois dans les zones intertidales et dans les zones profondes, alors que l'action érosive est principalement concentrée dans les zones littorales et peu profondes. C'est néanmoins dans les zones littorales et prélittorales que l'action sédimentologique glacielle est la plus évidente et la plus substantielle. Dans la zone intertidale, les glaces abandonnent des quantités considérables de sédiments: sur les cordons littoraux, les bas de plage, les slikkes et les schorres (DIONNE, 1970). Sur les rives du Saint-Laurent par exemple, elles ont transporté des milliers de blocs cristallins de la côte nord à la côte sud (DIONNE, 1972b). Elles abandonnent aussi chaque année des radeaux de schorre (DIONNE, 1968a, 1968c, 1972a), de vase et de sable graveleux dans les diverses zones perturbant ainsi l'équilibre sédimentaire établi par les vagues et les courants. L'on trouve des radeaux de schorre et des îlots de vase sur les cordons littoraux sablo-graveleux; des îlots de gravier et des blocs erratiques dans les schorres et dans les slikkes vaseuses. Certains secteurs du littoral sud du Saint-Laurent sont suffisamment alimentés en débris glaciels pour qu'on ait nettement l'impression que les glaces constituent le principal agent de sédimentation, les vagues et les courants limitant leur action au remaniement des apports glaciels; ce qui a fait croire à plusieurs qu'il s'agissait de dépôts morainiques remaniés.

Outre les apports détritiques et organiques, les glaces peuvent déformer les couches des formations meubles. Plusieurs auteurs attribuent à l'action des glaces flottantes diverses turbations affectant les formations quaternaires (WRANGEL, 1839; GEIKIE, 1882; SALISBURY & ATWOOD, 1897; EMERSON, 1898; LAHEE, 1914; JOHNSTON, 1917; KINDLE, 1917; LEGGET & BARTLEY, 1953; TARR, 1935).

4. — PROTECTION

En plus d'exercer un rôle d'érosion, de transport et de sédimentation, les glaces offrent aussi, durant une partie de l'année, une protection efficace contre l'action des vagues, des courants et des agents biologiques. Dans les régions arctiques par exemple, les glaces entravent l'action des vagues et des courants durant 8 à 11 mois par année; ce qui se traduit par une évolution très lente des littoraux. Les formes littorales non directement liées à l'action des glaces flottantes mettent beaucoup de temps à se développer; le matériel des plages est mal classé et peu usé; les falaises sont rapidement fossilisées par des talus d'éboulis que ne parviennent pas à déblayer les vagues et les courants; les promontoires rocheux ne subissant qu'exceptionnellement l'assaut des vagues reculent très lentement; bref, la nappe glacielle fige le littoral et ralentit considérablement son évolution. Dans les régions moins froides, comme celle du Saint-Laurent, la saison glacielle s'étend sur une période de 4 mois, durant laquelle l'action des agents normaux (vagues, courants, marées) est profondément entravée et souvent stoppée pour une période totalisant entre 60 et 90 jours selon les secteurs.

REFERENCES

ADAMS, J., (1825), "Remarks on the Movement of Rocks by the Expansive Power of Freezing Water", *Amer. Jour. Sci.*, vol. 9, p. 136-143.

ANONYME, (1822), "On Certain Rocks Supposed to Move Without any Apparent Cause", *Amer. Jour. Sci.*, vol. 5, p. 34-37.

BANCROFT, J. A., (1902), *Ice-borne Sediments in Minas Basin, N.S.*, Nova Scotia Inst. Sci., Proc. & Trans. (Halifax), vol. 11, No. 1, p. 158-162.

BARROIS, C., (1877), "Note sur les traces de l'époque glaciaire en quelques points des côtes de la Bretagne", *Ann. Soc. Géol. Nord*, vol. 4, p. 186-204, 1 fig., et *Bull. Soc. Géol. France*, vol. 5, 3e ser., p. 535-537.

BELL, R., (1886), "On Some Points in Reference to Ice Phenomena", *Trans. Roy. Soc. Can.*, vol. 4, sect. 3, p. 85-91.

BIRD, J. B., (1967), "The Geomorphic Role of River, Lake, and Sea Ice", in *The physiography of Arctic Canada*, Baltimore, John Hopkins, p. 217-224, 2 fig.

BROCHU, M., (1961), *Déplacements de blocs et d'autres sédiments par la glace sur les estrans du Saint-Laurent en amont de Québec*; Ottawa, Étude géogr., no 30, 27 p., 11 fig. (français et anglais).

BUCKLEY, E. R., (1901), "Ice Ramparts", *Trans. Wisc. Acad. Sci.*, vol. 13, pt. 1, p. 141-162, 17 fig.

BUSCH, A., (1941), "Eisschub-Berge im Wattenmeer", *Natur und Volk*, vol. 71, No. 2, p. 70-74, 6 fig.

CAILLEUX, A., et HAMELIN, L. E., (1967), "Périglaciaire actuel sur le littoral du Bic (Bas Saint-Laurent)", *Cah. Géogr. Québec*, no 23, p. 361-378, 14 phot.

CAMPBELL, N. J., et COLLIN, A. E., (1958), "The Discoloration of Foxe Basin Ice", *Jour. Fish. Research Bd.*, vol. 15, No. 6, p. 1175-1188, 4 fig., 6 phot. h.t.

CAREY, S. W., et AHMAD, N., (1961), "Glacial Marine Sedimentation", dans G. O. RAASCH (éd.) *Geology of the Arctic*, vol. 2; Toronto Univ. Press, p. 865-894, 8 fig.

CARSOLA, A. J., (1954), "Microrelief on the Arctic Sea Floor", *Bull. Amer. Ass. Petrol. Geol.*, vol. 38, No. 7, p. 1587-1601, 7 fig.

CHALMERS, R., (1882), "On Erosion from Coast-ice and Floating Ice in the Baie des Chaleurs", *Trans. Roy. Soc. Can.*, vol. 1, sect. 4, p. 285-286.

CHARLESWORTH, J. K., (1957), "Geological Action of Sea-ice", in *The Quarternary Era*, vol. 1, p. 587-590, London, Edward Arnold.

COLLINSON, J. D., (1971), "Some Effects of Ice on a River Bed", *Jour. Sed. Petrol.*, vol. 41, p. 557-564, 15 fig.

CONOLLY, J. R., et EWING, M., (1965), "Ice-rafted Detritus as a Climatic Indicator in Antartic Deep-sea Cores", *Science*, vol. 150, No. 3705, p. 1822-1824, 2 fig.

COOK, F. A., (1959), "Revue des études canadiennes de périglaciaires", *Geogr. Bull.*, nº 13, p. 38-53, (anglais-français).

CRARY, A. P., (1956), "Arctic Ice Island Research", dans H. E. LANDSBERG (éd.), *Advance in geophysics*, vol. 3, New York, Academic Press, p. 1-41, 17 fig.

CREWDSON, G., (1904), "Ice-action on Windermeer", *Geol. Mag.*, vol. 1, p. 524-525.

DANGEARD, L., (1929), "Observations de géologie sous-marine et d'océanographie relatives à la Manche", *Ann. Inst. Océanogr.*, vol. 6, 295 p., 27 fig., 18 pl.

DAWSON, J. W., (1886), "Note on Boulder Drift and Sea Margins at Little Metis, Lower St. Lawrence", *Can. Record Sci.*, vol. 2, No. 1, p. 36-38.
— (1893), *The Canadian Ice Age*, Montréal, William V. Dawson, 201 p., 26 fig.

DEBENHAM, F. A., (1919), "A New Mode of Transportation by Ice: the Raised Marine Muds of South Victoria Land (Antarctica)", *Quater. Jour. Geol. Soc.*, London, vol. 75, pt. 2, p. 51-76, 4 fig., 2 pl. h.t.

DE LA MONTAGNE, J., (1963), "Ice Expansion Ramparts on South Arm of Yellowstone Lake, Wyoming", *Univ. Wyoming, Contr. Geol.*, vol. 2, No. 1, p. 43-46, 4 fig.

DIETZ, R. C., CARSOLA, A. J., BUFFINGTON, E. C., et SHIPEK, C. J., (1964), "Sediments and Topography of the Alaskan Shelves", dans R. L. MILLER (éd.), *Papers in Marine Geology*, (Shepard commemorative volume), New York, McMillan, p. 241-256.

DILLON, W. P., et CONOVER, J. T., (1965), "Formation of Ice-cemented Sand Blocks on a Beach and Lithologic Implications", *Jour. Sed. Petrol.*, vol. 35, No. 4, p. 964-967, 4 phot.

DIONNE, J. C., (1962), "Note sur les blocs d'estran du littoral sud du Saint-Laurent", *Can. Geographer*, vol. 7, n° 2, p. 69-77, 8 fig.

— (1968a), "Schorre Morphology on the South Shore of the St. Lawrence Estuary", *Amer. Jour. Sci.*, vol. 266, No. 5, p. 380-388, 1 fig., 8 phot.

— (1968b), "Morphologie et sédimentologie glacielles, côte sud du Saint-Laurent", *Zeitsch. f. Geomorph.*, Sp. Publ. n° 7, p. 56-84, 1 fig., 16 phot.

— (1968c), "Action of Shore Ice on the Tidal Flats of the St. Lawrence Estuary", *Maritime Sediments*, vol. 4, No. 3, p. 113-115, 10 fig.

— (1969a), "Erosion glacielle littorale, estuaire du Saint-Laurent", *Rev. Géogr. Montréal*, vol. 23, n° 1, p. 5-20, 1 fig. 16 phot.

— (1969b), "Tidal Flat Erosion by Ice at La Pocatière, St. Lawrence Estuary", *Jour. Sed. Petrol.*, vol. 39, No. 3, p. 1174-1181, 9 fig.

— (1969c), "Bibliographie annotée du glaciel: aspects morpho-sédimentologiques", *Rev. Géogr. Montréal*, vol. 23, n° 3, p. 339-349.

— (1970), *Aspects morpho-sédimentologiques du glacial, en particulier des côtes du Saint-Laurent*; Univ. Paris, thèse doct. 412 p., 17 fig., 246 photo. aussi: *Lab. Rech. Forestières* (Québec), Rapp. Infor., QF-X-9, 324 p.

— (1971a), "Érosion glacielle de la slikke, estuaire du Saint-Laurent", *Rev. Géomorph. dyn.*, vol. 20, p. 5-21, 19 fig.

— (1971b), "Polygonal Patterns in Muddy Tidal Flats", *Jour. Sed. Petrol.*, vol. 41, p. 838-839, 4 fig.

— (1971c), "Nature lithologique des galets des formations meubles quaternaires de la région de Rivière-du-Loup/Trois-Pistoles", *Rev. Géog. Montréal*, vol. 25, p. 129-142, 3 fig.

— (1972a), "Caractéristiques des schorres des régions froides en particulier de l'estuaire du Saint-Laurent", *Zeitsch. f. Geomorph.*, Sp. Bd. n° 12, p. ??, 21 fig.

— (1972b), "Caractéristiques des blocs des rives de l'estuaire du Saint-Laurent", *Rev. Géog. Montréal*, vol. 26, p. ??, 22 fig.

— (1972c), "Distinction entre stries glacielles et stries glaciaires", *Bull. Ass. Fr. Et Quater.*, vol. 9, p. ??, 4 fig.

— (1972d), "Ribbed Grooves in Mud Tidal Flats", *Jour. Sed. Petrol.*, vol. 42, p. ??.

— (1972e), "Micro-craters in Muddy Tidal Flats of Cold Regions", *Jour. Sed. Petrol.*, vol. 42, p. ??.

— et LAVERDIÈRE, C., (1972), "A "Polar" Beach from Mid-latitudes". *Can. Jour. Earth Sci.*, vol. 9, p. ??.

EMERSON, B. K., (1898), *Geology of Old Hampshire county, Massachusetts*, U.S. Geol. Surv., monograph No. 29, 790 p., 48 fig., 32 pl. h.t.

EMERY, K. O., (1949), "Topography and Sediments of the Arctic Basins", *Jour. Geol.*, vol. 57, No. 5, p. 512-521, 1 carte h.t.

ENGELN, O. D. von, (1918), "Transportation of débris by Icebergs", *Jour. Geol.*, vol. 26, No. 1, p. 74-81, 5 fig.

FAIRBRIDGE, R. W., (1966), "Sea Ice Transportation", dans *The Encyclopedia of Oceanography*; New York, Reinhold, p. 781-782, 2 fig.

FEYLING-HANSSEN, R. W., (1953), "Brief Account of the Ice-foot", Norsk Geogr. Tidssk., vol. 14, Nos. 1-4, p. 45-52, 4 fig.

FORCHHAMMER, J. G., (1877), "Nouvelles observations sur les surfaces striées et polies du Danemark", Bull. Soc. Géol. France, (2e ser.), t. 4, p. 1177-1184.

GEIKIE, J., (1882), The Great Ice Age, and its Relation to the Antiquity of Man, New York, Appleton, 545 p., 17 fig.

GILBERT, G. K., (1908), "Lake Ramparts", Sierra Club Bull., vol. 6, No. 4, p. 225-234, 4 fig., 2 phot.

GOLDTHWAIT, L., (1957), "Ice Action on New England Lakes", Jour. Glaciol., vol. 3, No. 22, p. 99-103, 1 fig., 4 phot. h.t.

GRANT, A. C., (1965), Distribution Trends in the Recent Marine Sediment of Northern Baffin Bay, Halifax, Bedford Inst. Oceanogr., Rept. 65-9, 74 p., 16 fig.

GREEN, H. G., (1970), "Microrelief of an Arctic Beach", Jour. Sed. Petrol., vol. 40, No. 1, p. 419-427, 14 fig.

GRIGGS, G. B., et KULM, L. D., (1969), "Glacial Marine Sediments from Northeast Pacific", Jour. Sed. Petrol., vol. 39, No. 3, p. 1142-1148, 6 fig.

GRIPP, K., (1963), "Winter-Phänomene am Meeresstrand", Zeitsch. f. Geomorph., vol. 7, No. 4, p. 326-331, 22 phot.

GUSTAFSSON, J. P., (1902), "Om stranden vid nagra smaladska sjöor", Geol. Fören. Förh., vol. 26, No. 1, p. 147-153.

HAMBERG, A., (1919), "Observations on the Movement of Lake Ice in Lake Sommen in 1918 and Remarks on the Geographical Distribution of Similar Phenomenon", Bull. Geol. Inst. Univ. Uppsala, vol. 16, p. 181-194, 7 fig.

HAMELIN, L. E., (1961), "Périglaciaire du Canada: idées nouvelles et perspectives globales", Cah. Géogr. Québec, no 10, p. 141-203, 16 fig.

HANSEN, A, K., (1948), "Ispresning i Tystrup Sø og Esrum Sø vinteren 1946-47 (Ice pressure in Danish Lakes"), Geogr. Tidssk., vol. 49, p. 67-72, 4 fig.

HELLAAKOSKI, A., (1932), "Jäänpuristuksesta Saimaan Lietvedellä talven 1932 Aikana", Fennia, vol. 57, No. 3, p. 1-19, 7 fig.

HELMERSEN, G., von, (1856), "Uber das langsame Emporsteigen der Ufer des Baltischen Meeres und die Wirkung der Wellen und des Eises auf dieselben", Bull. Acad. Imp. Sci., Ser. Phys.-Math., vol. 14.

HIND, H. Y., (1875), "The Ice Phenomena and the Tides of the Bay of Fundy", Can. Monthly Nat. Rev., vol. 8, p. 189-203.

HITCHCOCK, C. H., (1860), "Lake Ramparts in Vermont", Proc. Amer. Ass. Adv. Sci., vol. 13, p. 335.

HOBBS, W. H., (1911), "Requisite Conditions for the Formation of Ice Ramparts", Jour. Geol., vol. 19, No. 2, p. 157-160, 1 fig.

HOLGERSSON, S., et HJELMQVIST, S., (1929), "Impressningen pa ven 1929", Geol. Fören. Förh., vol. 51, No. 3, p. 435-441, 11 fig.

HOUGH, J. L., (1950), "Pleistocene Lithology of Antarctic Ocean-bottom Sediments", *Jour. Geol.*, vol. 58, No. 3, p. 254-260, 2 fig.

— (1956), "Sediment Distribution in the Southern Oceans Around Antarctica", *Jour. Sed. Petrol.*, vol. 26, No. 4, p. 301-306, 1 fig.

HUME, J. D., et SCHALK, M., (1964), "The Effect of Ice-push on Arctic Beaches", *Amer. Jour. Sci.*, vol. 262, No. 2, p. 267-273, 4 fig., 4 phot. h.t.

JARVIS, G., (1928), "Lacustrine Littoral Forms Referable to Ice Pressure", *Can. Field Naturalist*, vol. 42, No. 2, p. 29-32.

JENNINGS, J. N., (1958), "Ice Action on Lakes", *Jour. Glaciol.*, vol. 3, p. 228-229.

JOHNSON, D. W., (1925), "Role of Shore Ice in Shoreline Development", dans *The New England-Acadian Shoreline*, New York, John Wiley, p. 589-591.

JOHNSTON, W. A., (1917), "Pleistocene and Recent Deposits in the Vicinity of Ottawa", *Geol. Surv. Can.*, Memoir 101, 69 p., 8 pl. h.t.

JOYCE, J. R. F., (1950), "Notes on Ice-foot Development, Neny Fjord, Graham Land, Antarctique", *Jour. Geol.*, vol. 58, No. 6, p. 646-649, 2 fig.

KEYSERLING, A., (1863), "Notiz zur Erklarung des erratischen Phänomens", *Bull. Acad. Imp. Sc.*, serv. Phys.-Math., vol. 6, p. 191-195.

KEYSERLING, M. de, (1869), "Sur l'envahissement du golfe de Reval par les glaces flottantes", *Bull. Soc. Géol. Fr.*, t. 27, (2e ser.), p. 223-225.

KINDLE, E.M., (1917), "Déformation of Unconsolidated Beds in Nova Scotia and Southern Ontario", *Bull. Geol. Soc. Amer.*, vol. 28, p. 323-334, 8 fig.

— (1924), "Observations on Ice-borne Sediments by the Canadian and Other Arctic Expeditions", *Amer. Jour. Sci.*, vol. 7, (5e ser.), p. 251-286, 2 fig. h.t.

KOSHECHKIN, B.I., (1958), "Traces of the Activity of Moving Ice on Shallow Bottoms in the North Caspian", *Trudy Lab. Aérometod. Akad. Nauk SSSR*, vol. 6, p. 227-234.

KRAUSE, E., (1941), "Eisschub-Berge und ihre Geologische Bedeutung", *Natur & Vol*, vol. 71, No. 2, p. 74-78, 5 fig.

KROPOTKIN, P.A., (1869), "The Effects of Shore Ice in Revel Bay", *I.R.G.G.O.*, No. 5.

KURDYUKOV, K.V., (1957), "Perenos gornykh porod ozernym l'dom (Transport of rocks by lake ice)", *Priroda*, No. 1, p. 90-91.

LAHEE, F.G., (1914), "Contemporaneous Deformation: a Criterion for Aqueoglacial Sedimentation", *Jour. Geol.*, vol. 22, No. 8, p. 786-790, 3 fig.

LASKAR, K., et STRENZKE, K., (1941), "Eisschub an Ufern norddeutscher Seen und seine Wirkung", *Natur & Volk*, vol. 71, No. 2, p. 63-70, 7 fig.

LEFFINGWELL, E.K., (1919), *The Canning River Region, Northern Alaska*, U.S. Geol. Surv., Prof. Paper, No. 109, 251 p., 33 fig., 35 pl. h.t.

LEGGET, R.F., et BARTHLEY, M.W., (1953), "An Engineering Study of Glacial Deposits at Steep Rock Lake, Ontario", *Econ. Geol.*, vol. 48, p. 513-540, 17 fig.

LISITSYN, A.P., (1962), *Bottom Sediments of the Antarctic*, Amer. Geophys. Union, Antarctic Research, Geophs. Monogr., No. 7, p. 81-88, 5 fig.

LYELL, C., (1843), "On the Ridges, Elevated Beaches, Inland Cliffs and Boulder Formations of the Canadian Lakes and Valley of the St. Lawrence", London, Phil. Mag., et Jour Sci., vol. 23, p. 183-186.

— (1845), *Travels in North America in the Years 1841-2*, New York, Wiley & Putnam, vol. 2, 221 p. (cf. p. 83-84 et 146-147).

— (1846), "On the Packing of the Ice in the River St. Lawrence", Quater. Jour. Geol. Soc. London, vol. 2, p. 422-427.

— (1854), *Principles of Geology*, New York, Appleton, 834 p., 120 fig. 4 pl. h.t. (1re éd. 1930, London, J. Murray); (cf. p. 219-221 et 227-232).

— (1866), *Elements of Geology*, New York, Appleton, (6e éd.), 803 p., 770 fig., (cf. p. 145-148).

MARUSENKO, Y.I., (1956), "Deyatel'nost'L'da na beregakh rek (Ice action on river banks)", *Priroda*, No. 12, p. 91-93.

MILLER, J.A., (1966), *The Suspended Sediment System in the Bay of Fundy*, Halifax, Dalhousie Univ., thèse M.Sc. non publiée, xii + 105 p., 15 pl. h.t. et 82 fig. h.t.

MOORE, G.W., (1966), "Arctic Beach Sedimentation", dans N.J. WILIMOUSKY et J.N. WOLFE (éd.), *Environment of the Cape Thompson Region, Alaska*, Oak Ridge (Tenn.), U.S. Atom Energy Comm., Rept. PNE-481, p. 587-608.

— (1967), "Arctic Beaches", dans R.W. FAIRBRIDGE, *The Encyclopedia of Geomorphology*, New York, Reinhold, p. 21-22, 2 fig.

NANSEN, F., (1922), "The Strandflat and Isostasy", *Vidensk, Skr., Math. Natur. KL.*, No. 11, 313 p., 169 fig.

NEEDHAM, H.D., (1962), "Ice rafted Rocks From the Atlantic Ocean off the Coast of Cape of Good Hope", *Deep-Sea Research*, vol. 9, p. 475-486.

NICHOLS, R.L., (1953a), "Marine and Lacustrine Ice-pushed Ridges", *Jour. Glaciology*, vol. 2, p. 172-175, 2 fig.

— (1961), "Characteristics of Beaches Formed in Polar Climates", *Amer. Jour. Sci.*, vol. 259, No. 9, p. 694-708, 3 fig. 7 phot.

OWENS, E.H., et McCANN, S.B., (1970), "The Role of Ice in the Arctic Beach Environment", *Amer. Jour. Sci.*, vol. 268, p. 397-414, 5 fig.

PELLETIER, B.R., (1969), "Submarine Physiography, Bottom Sediments, and Models of Sediment Transport in Hudson Bay", dans P.J. WOOD et al. (éd.), *Earth Science Symposium on Hudson Bay*, Geol. Surv. Can., Paper 68-53, p. 100-135, 20 fig.

PELLETIER, B.R., et SHEARER, J.M., (1972), *Sea Bottom Scouring in the Beaufort Sea of the Arctic Ocean*, Papers, 24th Inter. Geol. Congress, Montreal 1972.

PETERSON, J.A., (1965), "Ice-push Ramparts in George River Basin, Labrador-Ungava", *Arctic*, vol. 18, No. 3, p. 189-193, 3 fig.

POPOV, E.A., (1959), "The Effects of Ice Bodies and Shore Ice on Coastal Dynamics", *Trudy Okenogr. Kom. Akad. Nauk SSSR*, vol. 4.

PRATJE, O., (1933), "Winterspuren am Frühjahrsstrande", *Natur & Museum*, vol. 63, No. 1, p. 10-21, 15 fig.

PREST, W.H., (1901), "On Drift Ice as an Eroding and Transporting Agent", *Trans. Nova Scotia Inst. Sci.*, vol. 10, No. 3, p. 333-344.

REINECK, H.E., (1956), "Wattenmeer im Winter", *Senckenbergiana lethaea*, vol. 37, p. 129-146.

REINHARD, H., (1955), "Eispressungen an der Küste, *Wiss. Zeitsch. Univ. Greifswald, Math.-Natur. Reihe*, vol. 5, Nos. 6-7, p. 667-675.

— (1958), "Ueber Wirkungen des Eises an der Küste", *Wiss. Zeitsch. Univ. Greifswald, Math.-Natur. Reihe*, vol. 8, Nos. 1-2, p. 135-141.

REX, R.W., (1955), "Microrelief Produced by Sea Ice Grounding in the Chukchi Sea, Near Barrow, Alaska", *Arctic*, vol. 8, No. 3, p. 177-186, 8 fig.

— (1964), "Arctic Beaches, Barrow, Alaska", dans R.L. MILLER (éd.), *Papers in Marine Geology* (Shepard commemorative volume), New York, Mac Millan, p. 384-400, 8 fig.

SALISBURY, R.D., et ATWOOD, W.W., (1897), "Drift Phenomenon in the Vicinity of Devil's Lake and Baraboo, Wisconsin", *Jour. Geol.*, vol. 5, No. 2, p. 131-147, 7 fig.

SCOTT, I.D., (1927), "Ice Push on Lake Shores", *Papers Michi. Acad.*, vol. 7, p. 107-123, 6 fig.

STANLEY, D.J., et COK, A.E., (1967), "Sediment Transport by Ice on the Nova Scotia shelf", dans *Ocean Sciences and Engineering of the Atlantic Shelf*, Philadelphia, Trans. Nat. Symp. Marine Tech. Soc., p. 109-125, 16 fig.

STANLEY, G.M., (1955), "Origin of Playa Stone Tracks, Racetrack Playa, Inyo County, California", *Bull. Geol. Soc. Amer.*, vol. 66, No. 11, p. 1329-1350, 5 fig., 2 pl. h.t.

SVERDRUP, H. U., (1931a), "The Transport of Material by Pack-ice", *Geogr. Jour.*, vol. 77, No. 4, p. 399-400.

— (1913b), "Drift-ice and Ice-drift", *Geogr. Annaler*, vol. 13, Nos. 2-3, p. 121-141, 3 fig.

— (1938), "Notes on Erosion by Drifting Snow and Transport of Solid Material by Sea Ice", *Amer. Jour. Sci.*, vol. 35, No. 5, p. 370-373, 1 fig.

TARR, R. S., (1897), "The Arctic Sea Ice as a Geological Agent", *Amer. Jour. Sci.*, vol. 3, (4e ser.), No. 15, p. 223-229.

TARR, W. A., (1935), "Concretions in the Champlain Formation of the Connecticut River Valley", *Bull. Geol. Soc. Amer.*, vol. 46, p. 1493-1534, 2 fig., 11 pl. h.t.

TRASK, P. D., (1932), "The Sediments", dans *The "Marion Expedition" to Davis Strait and Baffin Bay*, Scientific results, pt. 1, p. 62-81.

TYRRELL, J. B., (1910), "Ice on Canadian Lakes", *Trans. Can. Inst.*, vol. 9, No. 20, pt. 1, p. 13-21, 12 phot. h.t.

VARJO, U., (1964), "Uber Eisexpansion an der Bucht Rauanlahti des Sees Puruvesi", *Zeitsch. Geomorpho.*, vol. 8, No. 3, p. 370-377, 6 fig.

WAGNER, W. P., (1970), "Ice Movement and Shoreline Modification, Lake Champlain, Vermont", *Bull. Geol. Soc. Amer.*, vol. 81, p. 117-126, 5 fig.

WARNKE, D. A., (1970), "Glacial Erosion, Ice Drafting, and Glacial Marine Sediments: Antarctic and Southern Ocean", *Amer. Jour. Sci.*, vol. 269, p. 276-294, 2 fig.

WASHBURN, A. L., (1947), "Reconnaissance Geology of Portions of Victoria Island and Adjacent Regions, Arctic Canada", *Geol. Soc. Amer.*, Memoir 22, 138 p., 4 fig., 32 pl. h.t.

WEBER, J. N., (1958), "Recent Grooving in Lake Bottom Sediments at Great Slave Lake", *Jour. Sed. Petrol.*, vol. 28, No. 3, p. 333-341, 10 fig.

WOOD, J., (1825), "Remarks on the Moving of Rocks by Ice", *Amer. Jour. Sci.*, vol. 9, p. 144-145.

WRANGEL, L. von, et ENGELHARDT, G. von, (1839), *Reise längs des Nordküste Siberiens... 1820-24*, Leipzig.

WRIGHT, C. S., et PRIESTLEY, R. E., (1922), *Glaciology; British (Terra Nova) Antarctica Expedition 1910-1913*, London, Harrison, 581 p., 179 fig., 291 pl.

ZENKOVICH, V. P., (1967), *Processes of Coastal Development*, New York, Interscience Publ., 738 p., 328 fig., (cf. p. 169-178).

ZUMBERGE, J. H., et WILSON, J. T., (1953), "Effect of Ice on Shore Development" *Berkeley, Proc. 4th Conf. Coastal Eng.*, p. 201-206, 2 fig.

Disequilibrium Characteristics in Fluvial Networks: Denudation Rates for Lake Ontario Watersheds[1]

E. D. ONGLEY,
*Department of Geography,
Queens University*

INTRODUCTION

Implicit in much of the empirical and theoretical research into fluvial networks has been the assumption of casuality between network planimetric geometry and contemporary morpho-climatic parameters.[1] While certain aspects of fluvial geometry has been clearly recognized as being of an hereditary nature (for example, DURY's (1964) work on meanders and underfitness) the imbalance between network form and particular hydrologic events has received only limited attention (GREGORY and WALLING, 1968; ROBERTS and KLINGEMAN, 1972).

MELTON (1957), considering that networks should reflect contemporary morpho-climatic influences, constructed a relationship between drainage density and the Precipitation-Effectiveness index. ONGLEY (forthcoming) examined networks in semi-arid Australia which are clearly relict, yet exactly obey HORTON's laws of drainage composition. These Australian networks, while essentially moribund for approximately ten thousand years, have not been effaced (ONGLEY, 1969). In general, while networks aggressively expand, their planimetric form cannot contract except by infilling. As a consequence, it would seem logical that the complexity of the network hierarchy represents a geometry formed in response to the most intense network-forming climatic regime experienced by the watershed during the period of its existence. It follows that contemporary networks, if not in equilibrium with contemporary climatic regimes and conditions imposed by land management practices, may be either expanding, or in a state of static disequilibrium. The latter possibility

[1] The methods and results of sediment yield studies are also reported in the *Canadian Journal of Earth Sciences*, Vol. 10, No. 2, 1973, pp. 146-156.

does not necessarily imply hydrologic inactivity; rather, it suggests an imbalance between form and process.

Abundant evidence exists to illustrate the imbalance between network form and process in areas used for agricultural purposes. Sediment loads have increased several-fold since forest clearing during colonial times. LIKENS et. al. (1970) found that controlled deforestation of an experimental water-shed in New Hampshire resulted in a six-fold increase in dissolved sediment load and a three-fold increase in inorganic particulate load.[2] Much of the particulate load was considered to be derived from channel beds and banks. While there exists a high rate of sediment loss for ploughed low-order basins, erosion is usually not producing a situation of drainage density transformation. Rather, the effect of ploughing, especially in areas of low relief, has often been to obliterate the natural low-order tributaries and to create new low-order channels which, while effective for draining ploughed land, bear no relationship to natural network-forming processes. In any case, whatever the nature of imbalance between network form and process, it would seem unlikely that networks in Southern Ontario would have achieved a new homeostasis in the short period since colonization.

Increased erosion with deforestation requires that care be taken in extending erosion rates, as calculated from modern sediment transport data, into the geological past. The presence or absence of non-arborial pollen (ragweed in particular) in Lake Ontario sediments (LEWIS and McNEELY, 1967) and bog deposits (TERASMAE, 1968), together with colonial records and C14 dating, may prove fruitful in establishing denudation rates in pre and post colonial times.

There appears to be three ways in which imbalance between network form and process may be manifest.

1. As indicated above, increased sediment transport may be, in large measure, related to agricultural disturbance; network form may no longer be related to contemporary (natural) network-forming processes, especially in the lower end of the Strahler-order spectrum where natural channels have been destroyed and artificial members created.

2. Accelerated erosion since deforestation may be extending contemporary networks through the processes of branching and head-

2 BORMANN and LIKENS (1970) report a nine-fold increase in particulate matter (organic plus inorganic) for he same study.

work growth. Certainly, in limited areas of Southern Ontario, there exists evidence for this growth behaviour.

3. It may be postulated that networks are overdeveloped for contemporary conditions, that is, networks are not representative of current climatic conditions. This third postulate presumes that the increase in sediment load is largely attributable to reworking of flood plain deposits in response to accelerated runoff and concomitant changes in fluvial regimes. The original network was, in large measure, either formed or modified to its present state in early deglacial times.

The third possibility was suggested to the writer by field observations during the periods of spring melt in unploughed low-order watersheds. Characteristically, low-order watersheds do not have discernible channels, yet clearly a considerable volume of sediment has been exported in order to produce each distinct watershed. Melt runoff, which appears to be the only kind of water exported in any quantity from these watersheds, seemed to be quite free of particulate material in those watersheds observed.[3] It has been shown (MELTON, 1957) that network growth occurs by creation of new low-order streams. Presumably, these same streams would be the first to 'decay' when network-forming conditions become less effective. However, because the low-order valleys exist, and cannot disappear except by complete infilling, they will continue to act as drainage units. Their decay is thus represented by non-erosion or negligible erosion. Hence, while low-order basins contribute significantly to the hydrologic characteristics of a watershed, they do not contribute materially to the denudation of a watershed. In this case, denudation rates derived from fluvial data may not apply to reduction of divides but to adjustment of flood plains to new climatic and cultural conditions.

In order to examine the question of inheritance in networks in Southern Ontario, two projects have been undertaken. The first, which forms the substance of this paper, is a background study for the purposes of establishing sedimentary parameters from water quality data for Canadian basins tributary to Lake Ontario. The second is a hydrometric investigation of two third-order networks on the Oak Ridges Interlobate Moraine, in which sediment transport is being examined within the hierarchical fluvial structure in relation to snow melt.

---

[3] Laboratory analysis of melt discharge is currently being carried out to test this field observation.

SEDIMENT DISCHARGE INTO LAKE ONTARIO
(CANADIAN DATA)

The study area is comprised of fifty-two (Canadian) watersheds tributary to Lake Ontario (Figure 1) and for which sediment data are available. This represents all watersheds of significant size and includes drainage systems varying from 1 mi.^{2} (2.59 km.^{2}) to

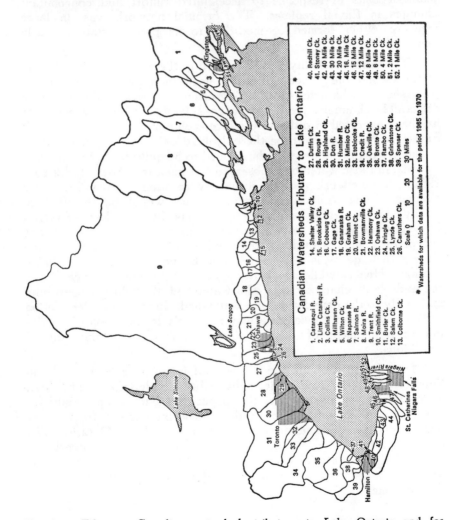

Fig. 1. — Fifty-two Canadian watersheds tributary to Lake Ontario and for which sediment data are available.

4,996.6 mi.² (12,941.2 km.², Trent River System). The Niagara River and the upper Great Lakes are not considered in this study.

The major physiographic features of the Lake Ontario watershed are illustrated in Figure 2. The larger networks between

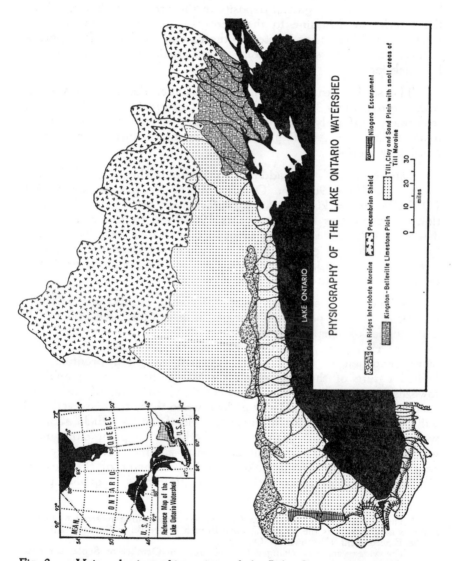

Fig. 2. — Major physiographic regions of the Lake Ontario watershed.

Niagara Falls and Oakville cut the Niagara Escarpment into numerous re-entrants and drain large areas of clay and till plains. Basins
between the Credit River and the Trent system flow southwards
from the Oak Ridges Interlobate Moraine across clay and till plains.
The Trent system drains a substantial area of the Precambrian
Shield and extensive glacial deposits in the area extending north of
the Interlobate Moraine to the Georgian Bay and Ottawa River
watersheds. The basins located to the east of the Trent flow across
a limestone plain with, in some cases, their headwaters on the
Precambrian.

The study area has a Dfb climate under the Koppen system,
with approximately 32 inches (812.8 mm) of precipitation distributed
reasonably uniformly throughout the year. A portion of the annual
total falls as snow, leading to high river stages during the March-
April melt period.

Data Sources. — In addition to data published (1966) for the
water year 1965-1966, the Ontario *Water Resources Commission*
(O.W.R.C.)[4] has kindly provided information on sediment load and
flow characteristics for water years 1965-1966 to 1970.[5] Sediment
determinations are made for suspended and dissolved loads only.
In view of shallow gradients and abundance of dams and weirs on
rivers in Southern Ontario, export of bedload from watersheds is not
thought by this writer to be particularly significant.

Sediment data are taken at approximately regular intervals; the
number of samples per water year per basin is illustrated in Table 1.
The number of samples per site is insufficient to derive a suspended
sediment rating curve. Indeed, because the O.W.R.C. is not primarily engaged in a systematic sediment sampling program, the
limited nature of the data obviously biases the following analysis
towards low flow conditions. Consequently, estimates of suspended
sediment load will undoubtedly be low, while those for dissolved load
will be excessive relative to suspended load values. Field samples
were collected by the 'grab sample' method at a point either mid-
way across the stream, or at the position of maximum flow. In either
case, the sample is usually taken within one meter of the surface.
On larger rivers or those with obvious differences in quality para-

---

[4] The Ontario Water Resources Commission data source referred to in this
paper is now known as the Water Quality Branch, River Basin Surveys, Ministry
of the Environment (Province of Ontario).
[5] The water year was changed in 1968 from an October to September base
to a calendar year base.

TABLE I

NUMBER OF SEDIMENT SAMPLES AND AVAILABILITY OF
DISCHARGE RECORDS PER BASIN PER WATER YEAR

Basin	1965-6	1966-7	1968	1969	1970
1. Cataraqui	6	12	16	12	11
2. L. Cataraqui	5	21	14	. 12	11
3. Collins Ck.	8	3	14	12	10*
4. Millhaven Ck.	9	3	10*	12*	11*
5. Wilton Ck.	8*	9*	14*	12*	11*
6. Napanee R.	7*	16*	18*	12*	12*
7. Salmon R.	6*	17*	19*	13*	11*
8. Moira R.	7*	10*	14*	11*	7*
9. Trent R.	7*	16*	19*	12*	10*
10. Smithfield Ck.	7	17	19	13	10
11. Butler Ck.	7	17	19	13	11
12. Salem Ck.	7	17	19	12	10
13. Colborne Ck.	7	17	19	13	11
14. Shelter Vly. CK.	6*	17*	18*	13*	8*
15. Brookside Ck.	5	17	17	13	8
16. Cobourg Ck.	8	17	19	13	10
17. Gage Ck.	6	17	18	13	9
18. Ganaraska R.	6*	17*	19*	13*	12*
19. Graham Ck.	6	17	19	13	11
20. Wilmot Ck.	6*	17*	19*	13*	11*
21. Bowmanville Ck.	6*	10*	20*	13*	11*
22. Harmony Ck.	6	16	19	13	10
23. Oshawa Ck.	6*	17*	19*	13*	11*
24. Pringle Ck.	6	16	19	13	11
25. Lynde Ck.	6*	15*	18*	13*	11*
26. Carruthers Ck.	9	25	29	22	18
27. Duffin Ck.	9*	24*	30*	12*	18*
28. Rouge R.	10*	24*	30*	22*	18*
29. Highland Ck.	8*	24*	30*	21*	18*
30. Don R.	9*	25*	30*	21*	18*
31. Humber R.	9*	25*	30*	22*	17*
32. Mimico Ck.	10*	25*	30*	22*	18*
33. Etobicoke Ck.	10	25*	30*	22*	18*
34. Credit R.	16*	14*	15*	10*	16*
35. Oakville Ck.	19*	22*	28*	18*	19*
36. Bronte Ck.	19	23*	29*	19*	17*
37. Rambo Ck.	18	24	29	19	20
38. Grindstone Ck.	19*	23*	29*	18*	20*
39. Spenser Ck.	20*	21*	31*	22*	21*
40. Redhill Ck.	7	19	31	22	22
41. Stoney Ck.	9	15	18	14	11
42. 40 Mi. Ck.	8	14	18	14	11
43. 30 Mi. Ck.	8	15	18	14	11
44. 20 Mi. Ck.	8*	15*	18*	14*	11*
45. 16 Mi. Ck.	7	15	18	14	10
46. 15 Mi. Ck.	8	15	18	14	10
47. 12 Mi. Ck.	9	14	18	14	11
48. 8 Mi. Ck.	6	13	18	14	11
49. 6 Mi. Ck.	7	14	18	14	10
50. 4 Mi. Ck.	8	16	18	14	9
51. 2 Mi. Ck.	6	14	18	13	9
52. 1 Mi. Ck.	8	13	18	14	10

*Federal gauge records available

meters, a composite sample is taken (J. RALSTON, personal communication).

Sediment load in tons per day may be calculated by multiplying daily mean sediment concentrations (suspended and dissolved) in grams per litre by the daily mean discharge in cubic feet per second; the product is multiplied by a conversion factor of 2.7. The O.W.R.C. calculates the average annual sediment load by averaging the individual sediment load values and multiplying by 365.

Flow data made available by the O.W.R.C. are usually taken from a federal gauge which may be some miles distant along the stream course. In a few instances flow data are recorded manually on site. Although sediment data provided by the O.W.R.C. are reliable, compilation of flow data by that agency is incomplete; hence, an approximation procedure (described below) is used to estimate annual mean flow.

The Water Survey of Canada maintains continuous recording gauges on 22 or more of the 52 basins used in this study. Table I lists the number of gauge records available per water year.

Analysis. — To allow for incomplete flow records from O.W.R.C. sources and to extend the analysis to basins for which only sediment data are available, an area-discharge equation was formulated from Water Survey records for those gauges within the study area. Log annual mean flow was regressed against log of basin area upstream of the gauge site for the period 1965-1966 to 1970. This relationship is expressed by

[1] Log_{10} Annual Mean Flow $= -.0213 + .9862\ \text{Log}_{10}$ Basin Area

$$n = 119 \qquad\qquad P_r < .01$$
$$r = +0.96 \qquad\qquad P\beta < .01$$

where n is the sample size, r is the correlation coefficient, and P_r and $P\beta$ express the significance of r and the regression coefficient β. Although the relationship is highly significant and the standard error small, the regression coefficients for yearly area-discharge equations were found to vary somewhat; hence, an estimating equation was established for each water year (Figure 3). By inserting the area upstream of the O.W.R.C. sample site, a reasonable value for annual mean flow per water year can be calculated for individual basins. With the data presently available, annual sediment load can be approximated by multiplying average annual sediment concentration by annual mean flow and multiplying the product by 2.7 and the number of days in the year. This procedure for determining annual sediment load from annual mean values of flow and sediment concentration is not identical to the O.W.R.C. method, whereby an annual value is calculated by averaging sampled loads. Hence, the degree of comparability of the two methods must be established.

The most direct way to compare total sediment load as computed by the O.W.R.C. from averaged daily values, and total load as calculated by annual mean values of flow and sediment concentration, is to compare the published O.W.R.C. annual load values (expressed in kilotons) with comparable values produced from the annual mean flow and sediment concentration data recorded by the O.W.R.C. Equations 2 and 3 respectively, indicate the comparability of the two methods for annual suspended and total sediment loads for the water year 1965-1966.[6]

Dependent Variable: Annual Suspended (or Total) Sediment Load per O.W.R.C.

Independent Variable: Annual Suspended (or Total) Sediment Load as calculated from annual mean values for flow and sediment concentration.

[2] Log_{10} Y(suspended) $=$ 0.0210 $+$ 1.0410 Log_{10} X(suspended)

$$n = 40 \qquad\qquad P_r < .01$$

$$r = +0.94 \qquad\qquad P\beta < .01$$

[3] Log_{10} Y(total) $=$ —0.0308 $+$ 1.0017 Log_{10} X(total)

$$n = 40 \qquad\qquad P_r < .01$$

$$r = +0.99 \qquad\qquad P\beta < .01$$

The variables n, r, P_r and $P\beta$ are as defined for equation 1. The relationships expressed by Equations 2 and 3 are highly significant, thus the procedure proposed for calculating annual sediment load yields annual sediment values comparable to those obtained by O.W.R.C. calculations. Nevertheless, as noted above, both methods are biased towards low flow conditions.

Table II lists the mean annual suspended, dissolved, and total sediment loads as calculated for the 5 water-year period 1965-1966 to 1970; the erosion rate expressed in feet per year is also tabulated for the 52 basins. Descriptive statistics for mean annual suspended, dissolved and total load for the 52 watersheds for the five water-year period appear in Table II. In each case, the data are right

---

[6] O.W.R.C. computation of annual loads is available only for the 1965-1966 period and does not include a value for annual dissolved load.

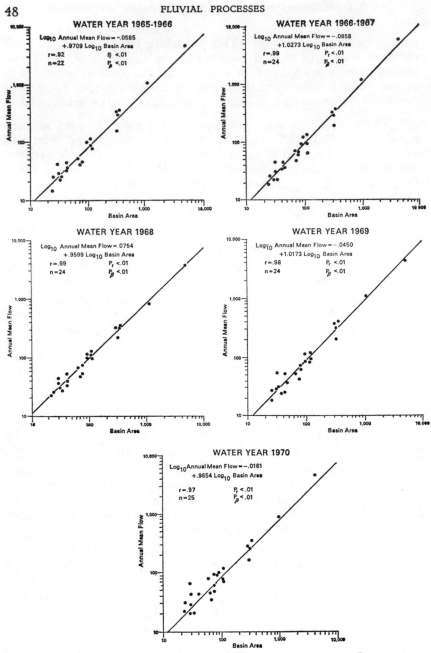

Fig. 3. — Estimating equations for annual flow per water year. Basin area is in square miles and annual mean flow in cubic feet per second.

TABLE II
MEAN ANNUAL SEDIMENT YIELD AND EROSION RATE PER BASIN

Basin	Mean Annual Sediment Yield (tons/year/square mile)			Erosion Rates (ft./year x 10^{-4})	Basin Area (square miles)	Mean Annual Flow (cfs)
	Suspended	Dissolved	Total			
1. Cataraqui R.	9.5	143.9	153.5	0.667	347.4	307.4
2. Little Cataraqui R.	12.5	289.5	302.0	1.313	27.4	24.9
3. Collins Ck.	7.9	229.0	237.0	1.031	63.9	57.5
4. Millhaven Ck.	7.1	201.7	208.8	0.908	56.7	51.1
5. Wilton Ck.	15.9	292.3	308.3	1.341	58.3	52.5
6. Napanee R.	12.2	169.3	181.5	0.789	323.0	286.0
7. Salmon R.	6.9	147.4	154.3	0.671	347.7	307.7
8. Moira R.	7.7	138.0	145.8	0.634	1096.5	960.2
9. Trent R.	8.5	138.1	146.6	0.638	4996.6	4322.5
10. Smithfield Ck.	14.5	266.6	281.1	1.222	10.4	9.5
11. Bulter Ck.	29.9	295.9	325.9	1.417	9.6	8.8
12. Salem Ck.	12.8	239.3	252.2	1.097	3.3	3.0
13. Colborne Ck.	26.1	253.9	280.0	1.217	18.9	17.2
14. Shelter Valley Ck.	22.4	254.8	277.2	1.205	25.3	23.0
15. Brookside Ck.	32.3	371.5	403.8	1.756	2.5	2.3
16. Cobourg Ck.	42.8	323.8	366.6	1.594	41.7	37.7
17. Gage Ck.	35.0	252.8	287.9	1.252	19.9	18.1
18. Ganaraska R.	22.9	215.5	238.4	1.037	101.0	90.5
19. Graham Ck.	46.5	240.0	286.6	1.246	29.1	26.4
20. Wilmot Ck.	36.6	313.9	350.5	1.524	33.2	30.1
21. Bowmanville Ck.	55.8	256.4	312.3	1.358	67.0	60.3
22. Harmony Ck.	28.5	384.1	412.7	1.794	36.7	33.2
23. Oshawa Ck.	33.8	396.1	429.9	1.870	49.6	44.8
24. Pringle Ck.	29.0	476.5	505.5	2.198	9.8	9.0
25. Lynde Ck.	34.6	314.0	348.7	1.516	53.1	47.9
26. Carruthers Ck.	26.2	324.5	350.8	1.525	10.8	9.9
27. Duffin Ck.	31.7	281.5	313.2	1.362	110.0	98.5
28. Rouge R.	29.9	334.3	364.2	1.584	146.3	130.6
29. Highland Ck.	73.2	606.0	679.3	2.954	34.9	31.6
30. Don R.	58.0	615.6	673.7	2.929	151.5	135.2
31. Humber R.	68.8	381.8	450.7	1.960	368.0	325.5
32. Mimico Ck.	46.5	642.0	688.5	2.993	33.6	30.4
33. Etobicoke Ck.	46.9	566.5	613.4	2.667	82.4	74.0
34. Credit R.	24.4	283.5	307.9	1.339	340.0	300.9
35. Oakville Ck.	29.0	289.4	318.4	1.385	149.3	133.2
36. Bronte Ck.	36.9	297.7	334.7	1.455	130.6	116.7
37. Rambo Ck.	36.5	570.7	607.3	2.641	5.4	5.0
38. Grindstone Ck.	55.1	384.3	439.5	1.911	51.9	46.8
39. Spenser Ck.	41.6	351.2	392.9	1.709	68.3	61.4
40. Redhill Ck.	49.5	469.8	519.3	2.258	19.5	17.8
41. Stoney Ck.	58.9	574.4	633.4	2.754	3.3	3.0
42. 40 Mile Ck.	42.9	584.8	627.8	2.730	29.3	26.6
43. 30 Mile Ck.	19.8	425.0	444.9	1.935	13.1	12.0
44. 20 Mile Ck.	22.8	436.7	459.6	1.998	137.2	122.5
45. 16 Mile Ck.	28.8	356.5	385.4	1.676	15.4	14.1
46. 15 Mile Ck.	23.5	368.9	392.4	1.706	13.3	12.2
47. 12 Mile Ck.	23.3	205.8	229.1	0.996	22.0	20.0
48. 8 Mile Ck.	17.6	367.7	385.3	1.676	2.1	1.9
49. 6 Mile Ck.	29.1	762.5	791.7	3.442	7.3	6.7
50. 4 Mile Ck.	29.8	533.2	563.1	2.449	12.0	11.0
51. 2 Mile Ck.	18.2	609.1	627.3	2.728	6.1	5.6
52. 1 Mile Ck.	29.0	415.6	444.6	1.933	1.0	0.9
Average	30.6	358.6	389.2	1.692		
Standard Deviation[2]	.260	.181	.181	$.0788 \times 10^{-6}$		

[1]predicted from area-discharge equation

[2]taken from $\log_{10}$ transformed values

skewed. Although log_{10} transformation reduces skewness, some poly-modality remains. The standard deviation recorded in Table II is obtained from the log_{10} transformed values.

Discussion. — On the basis of 168 stations throughout the United States, LANGBEIN and DAWDY (1964, p. D117) found that the proportion of total load carried as dissolved material increases with increasing humidity up to a point where, "...50 percent or more of the total load may be carried in solution...". While in this study the average dissolved component is 92% of the entire sediment load and has a mean concentration of 400 ppm compared with 143 ppm found by Langbein and Dawdy, the two observed values are un-doubtedly inflated as a result of sampling procedure. Nevertheless, the relative concentrations of suspended and dissolved material tend to follow the pattern found by LIKENS *et. al.* (1970) in New Hamp-shire. Bearing in mind that dissolved sediment yield is less depen-dent upon flow than is suspended sediment and therefore is not as sensitive to sampling bias, the mean annual dissolved load of 358.6 tons per square mile per year for the 52 basins is approximately three times larger than that predicted by Langbein and Dawdy for basins with a comparable mean annual runoff of approximately 12 inches. Undoubtedly, the high dissolved load component is, in part, attribut-able to the limestone and dolomite basement of most of the area, and to the carbonate content in the tills of Southern Ontario. Not-ably, the values obtained for tons of dissolved load per square mile are somewhat lower on watersheds located on the Belleville-Kingston limestone plain than for those found on deeper overburden. The spatial patterns of sediment discharge and denudation rates in Southern Ontario are currently under examination with respect to physical and cultural parameters.

Table II outlines denudation rates expressed in feet per year as calculated for the 52 watersheds. The data are right skewed and, although log_{10} transformation reduces skewness, polymodality is usual. The standard deviation recorded in Table II is obtained from the log_{10} transformed values. While an average value of .169 feet per 1,000 years corresponds to the mean denudation rate for United States basins with an effective precipitation of 30-40 inches as reported by SCHUMM (1963), the increased sediment discharge subsequent to colonization and deforestation in the past 200 years raises serious questions about the validity of historical extrapolation from the figures on Table II.

BRUNE, as reported in LANGBEIN and SCHUMM (1958), found that sediment yield per unit area decreases at a rate inversely proportional to the 0.15 power of basin area. While equation 4 expresses a similar relationship for Ontario data, only 26% of the variance is explained. It is likely that multicollinearity effects between area and relief will obscure any causality implicit in Equation 4. The relationships between area and relief,[7] and mean annual sediment yield in tons per mile (5 year period) are recorded below (Equations 4 to 9) for the 52 watersheds of this study. While several of the correlation coefficients are statistically significant, only a small

[4] Log_{10} Total Sediment Yield (tons mi.$^{-2}$) = 2.7589
               — .1304 Log_{10} Basin Area

    n = 52 P_r < .01
    r = —0.51 $P\beta$ < .01

[5] Log_{10} Suspended Sediment Yield (tons mi.$^{-2}$) = 1.5634
               — .0925 Log_{10} Basin Area

    n = 52   .05 <
    r = —0.25   .05 <
    P_r < .10
    $P\beta$ < .10

[6] Log_{10} Dissolved Sediment Yield (tons mi.$^{-2}$) = 2.7278
               — .1337 Log_{10} Basin Area

    n = 52 P_r < .01
    r = —0.52 $P\beta$ < .01

[7] Log_{10} Total Sediment Yield (tons mi.$^{-2}$) = 2.2735
               + .1864 Log_{10} Relief Ratio

    n = 52   .01 <
    r = +0.33   .01 <
    P_r < .02
    $P\beta$ < .02

[8] Log_{10} Suspended Sediment Yield (tons mi.$^{-2}$) = .7156
               + .4668 Log_{10} Relief Ratio

    n = 52 P_r < .01
    r = +0.57 $P\beta$ < .01

[9] Log_{10} Dissolved Sediment Yield (tons mi.$^{-2}$) = 2.2699
               + .1648 Log_{10} Relief Ratio

    n = 52   .02 <
    r = +0.29   .02 <
    P_r < .05
    $P\beta$ < .05

[7] Relief is recorded as a relief ratio which is a ratio between mean maximum height between basin mouth and divide, and the longest dimension of the watershed.

amount of the variance is explained; hence, other physical and cultural parameters must play an effective role in controlling sediment yield. Nevertheless, relative effect of relief and area on suspended and dissolved sediment yield merits attention. Dissolved sediment yield bears a closer relationship to area than to relief. On the other hand, suspended sediment yield is more closely associated with relief. The latter observation can be explained by the fact that suspended sediment is derived from surface erosion. Increasing relief is associated with larger energy environments with greater potential mobility of sediments. Dissolved load originates primarily from interflow and groundwater. While increased relief produces steeper groundwater gradients, dissolved load is less dependent upon relief than is erosion of particular matter.

Conclusions. — While networks grow in response to more intense network-forming conditions of a climatic and/or anthropomorphic nature, they do not decay except by infilling of channels. The abundance of low-order valleys without discrete channels and which export water only during the melt period may indicate the existence of networks which are overextended for today's conditions. Three heuristic models are presented to account for the possibility of an imbalance between network form and contemporary morphoclimatic conditions. It is convenient to commence a study of morphoclimatic imbalance by examining modern sediment yield data from Southeastern Ontario.

An approximate estimate of mean annual sediment inflow into Lake Ontario for fifty-two Canadian watersheds for the period 1965-1970 is obtained. Area-discharge relationships allow prediction of annual mean flow in ungauged watersheds for which sediment concentration data are available. Because of the nature of the data, mean annual sediment loads can be calculated only by use of annual mean values for flow and sediment concentration. Nevertheless, it is found that results obtained from this method are comparable to those values obtained by averaging daily load calculations and which are available in published form for one of the five water years under consideration. While the dissolved component of sediment load greatly exceeds that predicted on the basis of values reported for American watersheds, this observation may be, in part, attributable to sampling procedure. Although the mean denudation rate corresponds with that recorded for similar United States basins, questions are raised about the historical implications of the denudation concept in view of increased sediment discharge subsequent to deforestation during the colonial period of Southern Ontario.

Acknowledgements. — The writer wishes to express his appreciation to Mr. J. G. Ralston, Senior Engineer, River Basin Surveys (Ministry of the Environment), and the Water Quality Branch, Ministry of the Environment (Ontario) for making available unpublished sediment records, and to the Water Survey of Canada providing unpublished flow data. Mr. J. Lawrence performed the data computations. Funding provided by the Ontario Department of University Affairs is gratefully acknowledged.

REFERENCES

BORMANN, F. H., and LIKENS, G. E., (1970), "The Nutrient Cycles of an Ecosystem", *Scientific American,* 222, p. 92-101.

CHAPMAN, L. J., and PUTNAM, D. F., (1966), *The Physiography of Southern Ontario* (2nd edit.), Toronto, The University of Toronto Press, 386 pp.

DURY, G. H., (1964), *Principles of Underfit Streams,* U.S. Geol. Survey Prof. Paper, 452-A, 67 pp.

GREGORY, K. J., and WALLING, D. E., (1968), "The Variation of Drainage Density Within a Catchment", *Bull. Int. Assoc. Sci. Hydrology,* 13, pp. 61-68.

LANGBEIN, W. B., and DAWDY, D. R., (1964), *Occurrence of Dissolved Solids in Surface Waters in the United States,* U.S. Geol. Survey Prof. Paper, 501-D, pp. D115-D117.

LANGBEIN, W. B., and SCHUMM, S. A., (1958), "Yield of Sediment in Relation to Mean Annual Precipitation", *Trans. Amer. Geophys. Union,* 39, pp. 1076-1084.

LEWIS, C. F. M., and MCNEELY, R. N., (1967), "Survey of Lake Ontario Bottom Deposits", *Proc. Tenth Conference on Great Lakes Research,* pp. 133-142.

LIKENS, G. E., *et. al.,* (1970), "Effects of Forest Cutting and Herbicide Treatment on Nutrient Budgets in the Hubbard Brook Watershed-Ecosystem", *Ecol. Monographs,* 40, pp. 23-47.

MELTON, M. A., (1957), *An Analysis of the Relations Among Elements of Climate, Surface Properties, and Geomorphology,* Office of Columbia University, 102 pp.

ONGLEY, E. D., (1969), "A First Estimate of Absolute Age for Residual Soils in the Cobar Area of the Cobar Pediplain", *Australian Jour. Sci.,* 31, p. 432.

ROBERTS, M. C., and KLINGEMAN, P. C., (1972), "The Relationship of Drainage Net Fluctuation and Discharge", in ADAMS, W. P., and HELLEINER, F. M., (eds.), *International Geography 1972,* pp. 189-191.

SCHUMM, S. A., (1963), *The Disparity Between Present Rates of Denudation and Orogency,* U.S. Geol. Survey Prof. Paper, 454-H, 13 pp.

TERASMAE, J., (1968), "A Discussion of Deglaciation and the Boreal Forest History in the Northern Great Lakes Region", *Proc. Entomological Society of Ontario*, 99, pp. 31-43.

ONTARIO WATER RESOURCES COMMISSION, [n.d.], *Water Quality Data for Ontario Lakes and Streams*, Vol. II, 1965-66, Toronto, 364 pp.

—   (1968), "Drainage Basins in Southern Ontario, Map 1002-2, 1:1,013,760" Toronto.

WATER SURVEY OF CANADA, (1968), *Surface Water Data Reference Index, Ontario*, Inland Waters Branch, Dept. of Energy, Mines and Resources, Ottawa, 42 pp.

The Nature of Snowmelt Runoff Systems in Periglacial Terrain

J. G. Cogley,

S. B. McCann,
*Department of Geography,
McMaster University*

The paper read at the symposium explained the rationale and summarized the early results of a hydrological study being pursued on Cornwallis and Devon Islands, N.W.T., Canada. It is a Canadian contribution to the I.H.D., Project Number R-SR-21 N-11, with the title "Surface runoff of snowmelt and rainwater in the basin of the River Mecham, Cornwallis Island". The first full year of operation was 1971 after pilot studies took place in 1970, and it is planned to continue data collection in the field during summer 1972: it is possible that the program will be extended in 1973.

The basin of the River Mecham, which is approximately 90 km² in area, is large enough to provide a variety of ground conditions (relief and mantle material) yet small enough for ease of access: the narrow gorge just before the river reaches the sea provides an excellent site for stream gauging. The proximity to Resolute means that the basin is logistically suitable and that climatic data from a Grade A weather station are available for study. Annual precipitation is 136 mm, of which about half falls as rain between June and September. Temperatures are below freezing for nine months of the year, and the ground is in general permanently frozen, thawing in summer to depths of less than 1 m.

The project is an attempt to clarify some aspects of periglacial runoff systems, and to generate and test numerical hydrograph-based models of such a system. Historically the project originated with the realization, derived from the increasing familiarity of members of the Arctic Research Group with the physical environment of the area in question, that previous studies had underestimated the geomorphic significance of running water as a process in the periglacial landscape. This realization prompted the research con-

3

ducted in 1970 on south-west Devon Island and on the R. Mecham (see list of references), and led also to an appreciation of the fact that almost nothing was known, in quantitative terms, of the surface water hydrology of High Arctic regions.

The aims of the project, as conceived in 1970, are therefore three-fold:

i)

the clarification of problems associated with snowmelt and rainwater runoff over barren permafrost terrain, and the modelling of these processes: specifically, the modelling of the annual snowmelt flood, of diurnal fluctuations in snow-melt discharge and of basin response to rainstorms;

ii)

the assessment of rates of operation of fluvial denudation processes and the relative importance of these processes, and possibly backward extrapolation of these rates to help to derive a chronological sequence for the denudation of the area;

iii)

the study of processes of limestone solution, which are of particular interest in view of the lack of vegetation and presence of permafrost; these properties of the area offer an opportunity to test hypotheses, which have been the subject of recent controversy, concerning climatic and vegetational controls over limestone solution. These controls include the temperature-dependence of CO_2 solubility and the differing rates of CO_2 supply from organic and atmospheric sources.

The papers mentioned above report on the results of the reconnaissance phase of the work before 1971. The 1971 data collection program was successful in that a wide range of physical and chemical variables were monitored through the summer at the basin outlet, and spot measurements of discharge and water quality were made at sites of interest throughout the basin and in two neighbouring basins with denser cover of vegetation. Before reporting this information it is intended that the hypotheses formulated will be tested against the new 1972 data from the Mecham and hopefully from basins elsewhere in the eastern Arctic.

REFERENCES

COGLEY, J. G. *Hydrological and Geomorphological Observations on a High Latitude Drainage Basin: "Jason's Creek", Devon Island, N.W.T.*, M.Sc. thesis, Dept. of Geogr., McMaster University, 131 pp., 1971.

— Solutional processes in an arctic limestone terrain, *Spec. Publ. 4*, Inst. Brit. Geogr., 1972 (in press).

— and McCANN, S. B. Information on a snowmelt runoff system obtained from covariance and spectral analysis, *Trans. Amer. Geophys. Un.*, 52(4), 198 (abstr.), 1971.

McCANN, S. B. and COGLEY, J. G. Observations on water hardness from southwest Devon Island, N.W.T., *Can. Geogr.*, 15(3), 173-80, 1971.

— and COGLEY, J. G. Hydrological observations on a small arctic catchment, Devon Island, *Can. Jrnl. Earth Sci.*, 10, 1972 (in press).

— HOWARTH, P. J. and COGLEY, J. G. Fluvial processes in a periglacial environment: Queen Elizabeth Islands, N.W.T., Canada, *Trans. Inst. Brit. Geogr.*, 55, 1972 (in press); abstr. in *Area*, 3(1), 46, 1971.

Evolution de la teneur en produits dissous dans quelques cours d'eau des Cantons de l'Est, Québec

P. CLÉMENT,
Département de Géographie,
Université de Sherbrooke

ABSTRACT

Partial results are given, dealing with solute concentrations and yields in some Southern Quebec Appalachian streams, especially in the Eaton watershed. These streams generally flow on sedimentary and slightly metamorphosed rocks. Weak correlations between concentrations and discharge are observed, specially for anions, silica, total iron and magnesium, dilution not being the main factor. The role of local and seasonal influences is shown by spatial and time variations:

— lateral and bed erosion during floods yield relatively high contents in colloidal iron particles near pyrite rock exposures.

— biotic activity is responsible for concentration decrease during spring and summer for nitrates and silica; in the latter case this influence seems to be stronger in cultivated watersheds due to increased grass-covered surfaces.

The origin of some solutes is discussed: less than 5% according to erosion plot data comes from surficial runoff. High variation of silica yield during summer, not fully explained by discharge variation, seems to indicate that bed aquifers have lower contents than subsurficial side-slope water. Calcium, silica and nitrates yields for the whole Eaton watershed are respectively for 1969-1970 period about 9.5, 1.9 and 0.06 t/Km². Conclusion is drawn on the soil and subsoil column acting as a solute accumulator, periodically discharged by percolating water and partially controlled by biotic activity during the vegetative season.

Cet exposé est une partie d'un travail de plus vaste envergure dans le temps et l'espace, dont les objectifs sont l'évaluation de l'érosion chimique dans les Appalaches du Québec (Cantons de l'Est), les causes de ses variations temporelles et qualitatives et l'origine des produits dissous.

A. — LE TERRAIN

Les cadres sont un petit bassin hydrographique de 80 ha, situé sur le campus de l'Université de Sherbrooke et le bassin de la rivière Eaton (superficie d'environ 650 km²). Ils sont représentatifs des conditions naturelles et de leur transformation par les hommes (terrain mixte: forêts, pâturages et cultures)[1] [2].

GÉOCHIMIE DE QUELQUES ROCHES CONSTITUANTES (EN %)[3]

	SiO2	CaCO3 - CaO	MgCO3 - MgO	Fe2O3 - FeO
Calcaires	30–33	60–65	3–4	1–2
Schiste ardoisier	66	0–1	3	5
Grès, quartzites	65–80	1	1–3	3
Schiste à muscovite	50–76	0–8	1–5	6–8

Un till limoneux à limoneux fin en dérive et recouvre la majeure partie des bassins. La profondeur de décarbonation atteint 5 pieds[4].

Les relevés sont effectués avec une fréquence variant selon les conditions hydrologiques, augmentant lors des montées du niveau; en général, le rythme est d'ordre hebdomadaire sur six cours d'eau du bassin de l'Eaton, mais d'autres observations sont faites sur d'autres sous-bassins (carte, Figure 1).

B. — LES ANALYSES

Sur place sont mesurés température, conductivité, pH et teneur en oxygène dissous. Les autres déterminations sont faites au laboratoire de Géographie physique de l'Université de Sherbrooke selon les méthodes habituelles[5] en utilisant des produits préparés commercialisés. La reproductibilité des résultats est bonne, ainsi que la précision des titrages; les méthodes colorimétriques sont moins précises.

	CaCO3	SiO2
Reproductibilité (σ)	7%	5%
Erreur relative	3.5%	+ 20.5%

[1] L. CARTIER, A. LECLERC, (1964), *Rivière Eaton, caractéristiques topographiques du bassin-versant HP-5*, Ministère des Richesses Naturelles du Québec, 32 p.

[2] P. GADBOIS, (1970), "Contribution à l'étude d'un petit bassin versant (environs de Sherbrooke)", mémoire de maîtrise, Département de géographie, Université de Sherbrooke, 154 p.

[3] C. FAESSLER, (1962), *Analyses de roches de la Province de Québec, rapport géologique 103*, Ministère des Richesses naturelles du Québec, 1962, 251 p.

[4] B.C. McDONALD, (1969), *Surficial Geology of La Patrie-Sherbrooke Area, Quebec, including Eaton River watershed*, C.G.C., Paper 67-52, 21 p.

[5] A.P.H.S., (1970), *Standard Methods for the Examination of Water and Wastewater*, 13th Edition, 874 p.

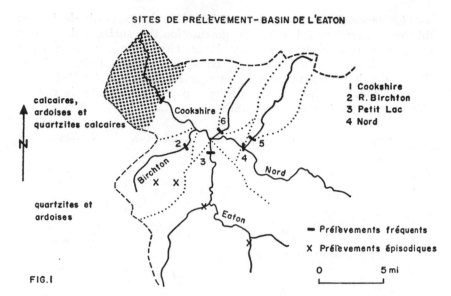

FIG. I

Les débits instantanés correspondant aux prises d'échantillons nous ont été fournis par le Ministère des Richesses Naturelles du Québec, que nous remercions.

C. — RÉSULTATS PARTIELS

Ils portent sur des observations allant de l'automne 1969 à l'été 1970.

1. RELATIONS DÉBITS — CONCENTRATIONS

Corrélations linéaires:

	$\overline{HCO_3}$	$CaCO_3$	$MgCO_3$	$\overline{Cl}$	Fer	SiO_2	$\overline{\overline{SO_4}}$	$\overline{NO_3}$
BIRCHTON	—0,66	—0,67	—0,17	0,01	—0,01	—0,30	—0,10	0,20
EATON (P. Lac)	—0,50	—0,57	—0,29	—0,17	0,46	0,26	—0,13	0,22
EATON (Cook.)	—0,55	—0,62	—0,33	—0,84	—0,00	—0,03	—0,07	0,71

Ainsi qu'il a été observé ailleurs[6], les corrélations sont faibles, sauf pour les produits les plus solubles excepté $MgCO_3$. Les diagrammes mettent en évidence certains faits:

[6] G.E. LIKENS, F.H. BORMANN, N.M. JOHNSON, D.W. FISHER, R.S. PIERCE, (1970), "Effects of Forest Cutting and Herbicide Treatment on Nutrient Budgets in the Hubbard Brook Watershed Ecosystem, Ecological Monographs", V. 40, 1, pp. 23-47.

— l'influence de la teneur en eau du sol et du sous-sol: le facteur dilution est tenu en échec par l'augmentation des surfaces de contact eau-composants minéraux et organiques, circonstance survenant par fortes pluies ou fonte des neiges. Ainsi pour HCO_3 (Figure 2), la diminution de concentration est plus rapide à faibles débits (inférieurs au débit moyen) alors qu'aux débits supérieurs la droite de régression tend à avoir une pente nulle.

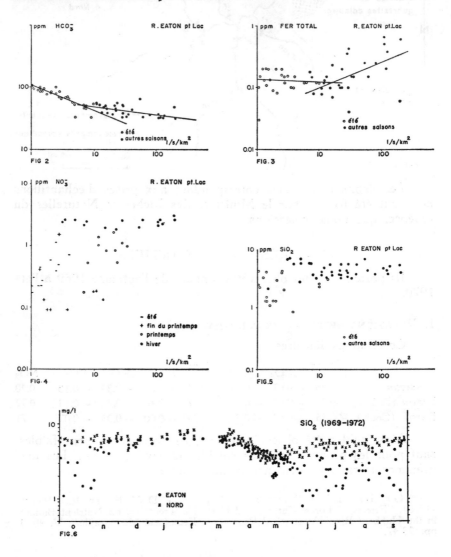

— le rôle des arrachages latéraux et de fond par temps de crue: les teneurs relativement élevées en fer total (fer dissous et particules colloïdales) s'observent sur les cours d'eau à proximité d'affleurements pyriteux lors des crues (Figure 3).

— la mobilisation de certains produits par la végétation et les organismes du sol: l'exemple le plus net est celui des nitrates (Figure 4) pour lesquels un groupement saisonnier apparaît. Les plus basses concentrations de fin de printemps correspondent à la pleine activité végétale où les plantes utilisent les nitrates du sol au maximum, libérés par contre par les eaux hivernales. Les concentrations en silice n'obéissent pas aux variations du débit (Figure 5); cependant on observe une diminution en avril et mai (Figure 6), surtout sur l'Eaton à Petit Lac. Or, ce sous-bassin possède par rapport à son voisin de la rivière du Nord des superficies plus élevées en pâturages et cultures; on sait que les plantes annuelles herbacées fixent de la silice lors de leur pousse printanière, silice relâchée à la morte-saison.

2. Origine des produits exportés

Le rôle de la lithologie apparaît dans le tableau suivant; les équations des droites de régression expriment les relations dégradation spécifique en $mg/s/km^2$ par produit — débit spécifique en $1/s/km^2$. Voir tableau I.

	Ca^{++}	SiO_2
Birchton	$\log Dgs = 1,68 + 0,76 \log Ds$	$= 0,76 + 0,87 \log Ds$
Eaton (P. Lac)	$\log Dgs = 1,47 + 0,74 \log Ds$	$= 0,36 + 1,13 \log Ds$
Eaton (Cookshire)	$\log Dgs = 1,54 + 0,72 \log Ds$	$= 0,54 + 1,01 \log Ds$

Note: Les deux derniers cours d'eau possèdent une majorité de roches siliceuses.

La part des affluents de l'aval comportant des calcaires dans leur bassin est sensible lors des bas débits sur l'Eaton à Cookshire; elle diminue lors des forts débits, comme l'indique le croisement des droites de régression de l'Eaton à Cookshire et Petit Lac (Figure 7).

Le ruissellement superficiel ne participe à l'exportation de la charge dissoute que pour une faible part, si on étend les observations de nos parcelles expérimentales[7]. Pour Ca^{**}, Mg^{**}, SiO_2, SO_4, le

[7] P. Clément, (1971), *Exportation de produits dissous par les eaux de ruissellement superficiel, Communication au 39e Congrès de l'A.C.F.A.S.*, Sherbrooke.

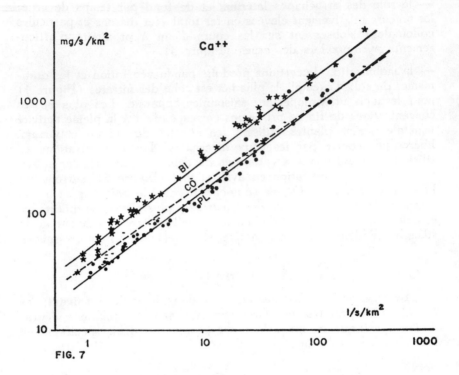

FIG. 7

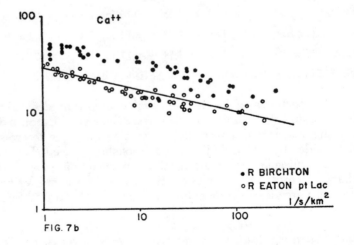

FIG. 7 b

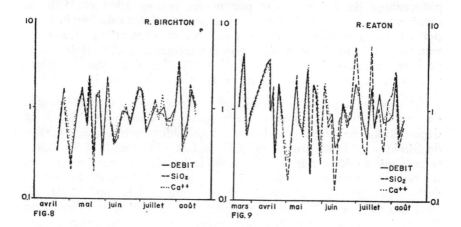

FIG.8

FIG.9

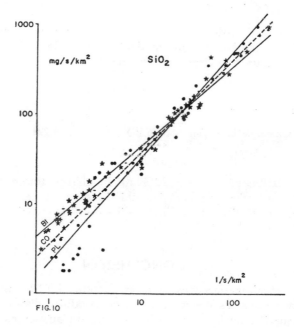

FIG.10

pourcentage du poids évacué par la surface en 1969 et 1970 ne représente que 1 à 5% du total évacué par le ruisseau du bassin comportant ces parcelles. D'autre part, les concentrations des eaux recueillies à la sortie de drains sous ces mêmes parcelles étaient très proches de celles du ruisseau. La contribution des eaux hypodermiques et du contact avec la roche en place est donc l'essentiel.

Certaines hypothèses peuvent être émises quant à l'origine exacte de certains produits. Durant le printemps, débits spécifiques et dégradations spécifiques varient de façon identique sur le ruisseau de Birchton et la rivière Eaton à Petit Lac (Figures 8 et 9). Ceci se poursuit en été sur le premier, dont le bassin est constitué par du till recouvrant la roche. À Petit Lac, les variations de la dégradation spécifique en silice oscillent plus que le débit spécifique; les eaux des nappes du lit, qui soutiennent les bas débits, semblent donc être moins chargées en silice que celles issues des terrasses et des versants latéraux, qui concourent aux forts débits.

3. Quantités évacuées

Le tableau ci-dessous donne quelques valeurs pour l'Eaton à Cookshire en se basant sur un débit moyen de 12,900 l/s, soit un débit spécifique d'environ 20 l/s/km² [8].

		Ca	SiO$_2$	$\overline{NO_3}$
EATON	t. par km²/an	9.46	1.90	0.06
	t. pour le bassin/an	6,100	1,224	41
CAMPUS	t. par km²/an	3.7 à 5.2	1.1	0.22

En attribuant à CA** 20% de la charge totale dissoute, une estimation grossière de l'érosion chimique serait de 50 t/km²/an et de 30,000 t. environ pour la totalité dans le bassin de la rivière Eaton.

CONCLUSION

Ces résultats montrent que le facteur dilution ne joue qu'un rôle effacé dans les concentrations en produits dissous. L'essentiel de l'évacuation de la charge dissoute est dû aux crues saisonnières,

---

[8] D.H.Q.-2, *Rivière Eaton, Débits journaliers 1932-1964*, Ministère des Richesses naturelles du Québec, 53 p.

notamment celle de printemps. Pour celle-ci, on observe une baisse de concentrations après une première phase; la tranche de terrains où circulent les eaux est assimilable à un accumulateur d'éléments solubles, préparés par les actions météoriques antérieures, que la percolation active printanière décharge. À ce moment, toute la colonne contribue à l'évacuation. Plus tard, les différenciations apparaissent, selon les profils d'humidité et les emmagasinages d'origine biotique. La connaissance de ces phénomènes est donc nécessaire à la construction de modèles de l'érosion chimique dans un bassin hydrographique.

REMERCIEMENTS

Nous remercions le Comité consultatif national de la Recherche géographique et le ministère de l'Éducation du Québec pour les subventions qui ont permis ces travaux.

Tableau 1. — ÉPREUVES DE SIGNIFICATION.

		N.obs	r	t	s	t. de b
BIRCHTON	(Ca^{++}).	46	0,935	17,6	0,191	17,9
	(SiO$_2$).	46	0,932	17,1	0,224	17,5
EATON	(Ca).	61	0,933	19,9	0,184	20,3
PT LAC	(SiO$_2$).	61	0,960	26,2	0,214	27,3
EATON	(Ca^{++}).	23	0,992	36,8	0,056	29,4
COOKSHIRE	(SiO$_2$).	23	0,985	26,7	0,110	27,3

r :— Cœfficient de corrélation.

s :— Erreur-type de l'estimé de y.

b :— Cœfficient de régression.

NOTE: Pour Birchton et Pt. Lac, observations d'avril 1969 à août 1970; pour Cookshire, d'avril 1970 à août 1970.

Some Preliminary Investigations of the Canyons of the South Nahanni River N.W.T.

D. FORD,
Department of Geography,
McMaster University

ABSTRACT

The South Nahanni River flows E to the Liard and the Mackenzie and in the lower portion of its passage through the Mackenzie Mountains, drops over Virginia Falls, (—294 feet), and then passes through three great canyons. The canyons have an incised meander form with several cut-off hairpin meanders. Local relief in the canyons is generally 2000-3000 feet. The mean gradient of the River through them is 12 feet per mile: it is without bedrock rapids though there are riffles where it is constricted by delta-building from tributary canyons. The River is very turbid and moves a substantial bedload of medium-sized boulders and smaller particles.

First Canyon is furthest downstream and thus base level for the others. In its eastern half it is entrenched into 800 feet of limestone, (Nahanni Formation of Devonian age), and 3000 feet of dolomite beneath. Strata dip regularly eastwards, (downriver), at 10°. Superincumbent shales have been stripped from the limestone to leave extensive stratimorphic plateaus flanking the canyons. Subterranean drainage from the plateaus towards the River has created a series of caverns in the limestone. They are of the shallow subwatertable type, now drained and fossilised. Drainage was a consequence of the River entrenching below the spring positions. Preliminary U-Th. dating of the first stalagmite deposited after drainage has yielded ages of 275,000 years or more. From this, the mean maximum rate of River entrenchment in First canyon has been 2.66 feet per 1000 years for the 275,000 year period. Extrapolating the rate, the age of the three South Nahanni canyons is placed broadly at 1.1 million years B.P.

The canyon region escaped the Last Glaciation though it has certainly been glaciated at least once. Some problems of the erasure of glacial erosion forms by fluvial activity are considered. The S Nahanni canyons meander but most tributary canyons are quite straight. Implications of this contrast are discussed.

Complex Drainage System Response to Altered Baselevel

R. S. PARKER,
Department of Geology,
Colorado State University

Problems of correlating alluvial deposits for developing Pleistocene alluvial chronologies (SCHUMM, 1965) and problems associated with gully and arroyo control are both made more difficult by the lact of understanding of the mechanics of valley-fill trenching and deposition. The response of a drainage basin to changes in such external variables as climate or baselevel may produce a more complex response than is usually realized.

The results of an experimental study of drainage pattern development and evolution provide some insight into the complexity of valley-fill trenching and deposition. It is the purpose of this paper to demonstrate that the response of a drainage system to changes of external variables will be a complex sequence of erosion and deposition within the channel system.

EXPERIMENTAL DESIGN

An experimental facility, designed for a study of the interrelations between drainage basin morphology and hydrologic response, provides a unique opportunity to study the evolution of a drainage system. The 9.2 by 15.2 m. container was filled to a depth of 1.5 m. with a mixture of sand, silt, and clay. The material contained approximately 28 percent silt-clay to provide a moderately cohesive mixture within which channels could form and valley sides develop. Artificial precipitation with a maximum intensity of nearly 7 cm/hr could be applied to the surface by a series of sprinklers along the sides of the container (HOLLAND, 1969).

An experiment was designed to document the evolution of a drainage pattern on a smooth, relatively flat surface. Thus, the

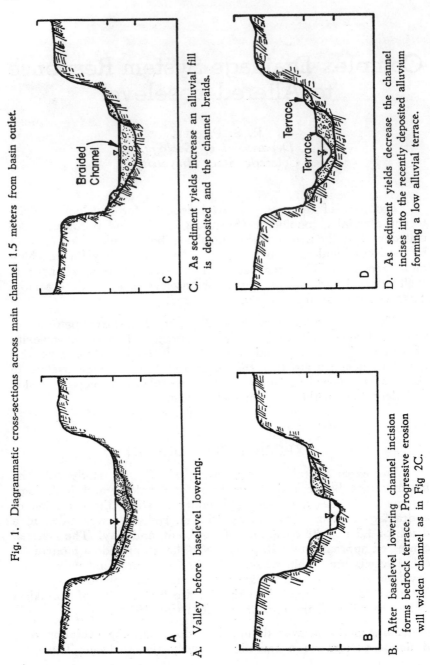

Fig. 1. Diagrammatic cross-sections across main channel 1.5 meters from basin outlet.

A. Valley before baselevel lowering.

B. After baselevel lowering channel incision forms bedrock terrace. Progressive erosion will widen channel as in Fig 2C.

C. As sediment yields increase an alluvial fill is deposited and the channel braids.

D. As sediment yields decrease the channel incises into the recently deposited alluvium forming a low alluvial terrace.

surface was graded into two intersecting planes with a maximum slope of 0.75 percent toward the outlet. In order to initiate erosion, base-level at the outlet was lowered ten centimeters and the maximum precipitation rate (7 cm/hr) applied for several hours. Sediment samples were taken every half hour at the outlet and the network documented as evolution continued.

After ten hours, the growth of the network had essentially ceased. This was indicated by little change in the network pattern and by the reduced and nearly constant value of the sediment yield. In order to renew erosion on the watershed surface and allow the pattern to continue its extension on the undissected upland, it was necessary to lower the baselevel another ten centimeters.

After a period of time, the network again essentially stopped its headward growth, and in order to rejuvenate the system the base-level was again lowered. This sequence of base-level lowerings was repeated five times (runs) until the drainage system filled the available space in the experimental basin.

BEHAVIOR OF MAIN CHANNEL
FOLLOWING INCISION

The initial base-level lowering produced a drainage pattern in the lower half of the basin. This network had 124 first order streams and the main channel at the outlet had a Strahler order of five. After the first run, a sequence of erosional and depositional events were observed in the main channel each time the base-level was lowered. This sequence was difficult to document quantitatively but the sequence can be depicted in a series of conceptual cross-sections based on measurements made on the channel 1.5 m. from the mouth of the basin (Fig. 2).

Figure 2A shows the cross-section of the channel at the end of the first run before base-level was lowered again. Sediment yields have declined and the system has essentially stopped headward growth. The channel at this time is carrying a much reduced sediment load.

Renewed downcutting of the main channel following rejuvenation is shown in Figure 2B shortly after the knickpoint has passed the cross-section. One can identify bedrock terraces that are associated with the change in base-level. The width-depth ratio is small and the channel is fairly straight.

The knickpoint or zone of maximum erosion continues its migration upstream and encounters more tributaries. This upstream migration of erosion increases the sediment delivery to the point in the main channel under observation, thereby causing the stream to braid and deposit alluvial material. At the same time the main channel increases its sinuosity and the lateral migration erodes parts of the bedrock banks. Figure 2C shows the result of the lateral migration of the channel and the deposition of alluvial material. The width-depth ratio has increased substantially.

As the zone of maximum erosion extends to the sources, sediment yield declines. With less sediment delivery to the cross-section on the main channel, the stream incises into the alluvial fill, decreasing its width-depth ratio (Fig. 2D). This secondary incision forms an alluvial terrace. Two terraces are identified in Figure 2D. One, the bedrock terrace formed during initial incision and, two, an alluvial terrace formed by changes in sediment delivery to the cross-section.

The identification of sediment load changes at the point where the cross-sections were taken is complicated by lateral migration of the main channel, associated bank caving, and the accumulation of alluvial material in the valley. These additional variables tend to increase alluvial material at the cross-section causing an increase in depth of alluvial fill.

CONCLUSIONS

W. V. LEWIS (1944) conducted an experiment in which a tributary system was initially cut into material on a stream table. Water fed into the tributaries produced terraces in the lower reaches of the main channel without any corresponding change of sea level, tilt, or discharge. Lewis summarized the development of the terraces as follows:

1) A rapid supply of material to the streams when slopes were steep and new channels were being cut,

2) building of steep gradients in the flood plain for the transportation of this heavy load,

3) a reduction in the supply of material as slopes upstream become more gentle and the stream courses were stabilized,

4) a corresponding reduction of gradient in the flood plain owing to much reduced load carried seawards,

5) the stream consequently cut into its former terraces.

Hence, not only a base-level change but any event which causes rejuvenation of a channel system such as a climate change will produce a complex response. It appears that an event that causes an erosion response within a drainage basin automatically creates a negative feedback (high sediment production) which causes deposition. This type of natural situation has been suggested as typical of the arroyo cycle in New Mexico as well as in other Southwestern channels (SCHUMM and HADLEY, 1957). The Rio Puerco in New Mexico, although trenched to depths of 12.2 m. upstream is now only 3.7 m. deep near its mouth; the result of deposition of some very high sediment loads that are moved through this channel.

Figure 2 summarizes the erosion-deposition sequence in time at only one location in a stream system. The complexity of this sequence is increased by the fact that it will occur at different times in different locations along a channel system.

Such a complex relation among cut-fill sequences in Holocene deposits in which inset fills are the result of upstream tributary rejuvenation may be part of the reason why recent stratigraphic correlations are difficult.

Certainly, more attention needs to be placed on this complex cycle when utilizing gully control works (SCHUMM, 1969). Successful control structures probably work within the cycle of erosion and aggradation to enhance portions of the natural sequence in order to control gullying. Structures, evaluated as ineffective, may be correctly designed but ineffectively placed with regard to the natural cycle. For example, a structure placed in a degrading reach has less ability to improve aggradation. More economical structures could be employed to enhance deposition in an aggrading reach. Indeed, better economic evaluation of control systems may well be possible by understanding this natural cycle.

As more experimental and process-oriented studies of ephemeral stream channels are made, it is believed that a principle of complex response will be established. That is, in a natural system one event can trigger a complex morphological and stratigraphic response. This principle may provide a partial explanation of the complicated sequence of events produced in response to a change in an external variable such as climate or base-level.

REFERENCES

HOLLAND, M. E., (1969), *Colorado State University experimental rainfall-runoff facility: Design and testing of rainfall system,* Colo. State Univ. Eng. Res. Center (Ft. Collins), CER 69-70 MEH21.

LEWIS, W. V., (1944), "Stream through experiments and terrace formation" *Geol. Magazine,* V. 81, p. 241-252.

SCHUMM, S. A., (1965), "Quaternary Paleohydrology", in H.E. WRIGHT, Jr. and R. B. MORRISON, eds. *The Quaternary of the United States,* Salt Lake City, Univ. Utah Press, p. 591-631.

— (1969), "A geomorphic approach to erosion control in semiarid regions", *A.S.A.E., Trans.,* p. 60-68.

SCHUMM, S. A., and HADLEY, R. F., (1957), "Arroyos and the semiarid cycle of erosion", *Amer. Jour. Sci.,* V. 255, p. 161-174.

Channel Morphology
and Dispersion Effects in Streams

R. G. WARNOCK,
Department of Civil Engineering,
University of Ottawa

Recent interest in the processes of dispersion in streams has arisen primarily from the study of two problems. One of these is the study of the spreading of pollutants introduced into streams. The other one is the study of the dispersion of suspended sediments which are picked up and carried in the stream. This paper is based upon data collected on the Ottawa River as part of a larger study of the river and the effect of pollutants upon it.

The region of the river under consideration is shown in Figure 1. Within this reach the Gatineau River, a major tributary, joins the Ottawa. Also, several islands affect the distribution of flow. These factors affect the dispersion processes in the river. It is the purpose of this paper to examine these effects. First the effects of the mixing zone will be considered; then the role of islands will be discussed.

Numerous studies have been made in the past of shear flows similar to this one. Perhaps the most pertinent one is a study conducted by Pratte and Baines[1] of a round jet discharging into a cross flow. They found that the profiles of jets of different size and velocity could be correlated well by using the ratio of jet velocity to cross flow velocity and the initial jet size as parameters. The most seriously limiting factor in their study as it applies to this case is that they assumed the jet velocity to be much greater than the cross flow velocity.

The most commonly used method of measuring dispersion in a river is by the use of a tracer put into the flow. Rhoda mine-B dye, a fluorescent dye, was used in this study for this purpose.

---

[1] B.D. PRATTE, and W.D. BAINES, "Profiles of the Round Turbulent Jet in a Cross Flow", *Journal of the Hydraulics Division*, ASCE, Vol. 94, No. HY6, Proc. Paper 5556, Nov. 1967, pp. 53-64.

However, the Ontario Water Resources Commission requested that any use of dye conform to the new standards for effluents into the river, particularly in regard to color. This seriously limited the amount of dye that could be used at any one time and it was found in the study of the river in the Ottawa-Hull area that the method, under this restriction, would not give useful results.

After the results of the dye test were found to be inconclusive for this part of the river, a water quality parameter was sought which would be of sufficiently different magnitudes in the two rivers so that the mixing zone could be defined by it. It was found that, due to the effluent from the E. B. Eddy mill in Hull, there was a high level of fluorescence in the Ottawa River downstream. Accordingly in a preliminary trial of the method the fluorescence was measured across several transverse sections upstream and downstream of the mouth of the Gatineau. These sections are numbered 1 through 5 on Figure 1. The fluorescence levels for these sections are shown on Figure 2. The results from this trial show a rapid lateral diffusion in the mixing zone. It is hoped that further measurements by this method may be made.

During spring runoff the Gatineau River carries a much larger suspended sediment load than the Ottawa at this part of the river. This fact was observed from a series of air photographs of the region taken in April 1971, in which the boundary between the flows of the two rivers is clearly discernible for several thousand feet below the confluence. These photos were used to locate the boundary of the mixing zone. The results of this study are plotted in Figure 3. These show the profiles of the boundary on 6 different days. The ratio of the flow rate in the Ottawa to that in the Gatineau is shown for each day. The flow rates used are daily average values.

It can be seen that the profiles fall into two groups. In the upper group the ratio of flows are 4.3, 4.3 and 5.0. In the lower group the ratios are 3.5, 6.8 and 11.7. The value of 3.5 was obtained, however, at a considerably lower flow rate (38,900 cfs) in the Ottawa River than for any other day the next lowest value being 50,000 cfs. Thus, a tentative conclusion is that the boundary profiles are related to the rate of flow in the main stream as well as the ratio of flows between the main stream and the tributary. This is at variance with the study of Pratte and Baines. However, in their study the jet flow velocity was 5 times the velocity of the cross flow or more.

Another fact which should be noted is that when the boundary occurs near the center of the stream it appears to be affected by the expansion in the channel which occurs below the confluence of the two streams. This is evidenced in Figure 3 by the upward con-cavity of the profiles in the upper group. This phenomenon enhances the transverse mixing as the zone of a flow expansion is a region in which considerable turbulent mixing will occur.

In conclusion it is seen that the inflow of a tributary causes increased lateral mixing and that this mixing may be affected by the downstream geometry.

In order to assess the influence of islands on the dispersion of material, Taylor's[2] equation for a steady uniform one-dimensional flow is used. This equation, which was developed for pipe flow, has been widely used in the study of dispersion in rivers and estuaries despite its theoretical limitations. Longitudinal dispersion is due mainly to the velocity variation across the flow. It is represented by the longitudinal dispersion coefficient, D_L. To understand its physical meaning, consider the movement of a sluf of tracer material down a river as viewed from a frame of reference moving at the mean velocity. The concentration of material would decrease both up and downstream from a peak value in a manner approximated by a normal effort curve. As the cloud moves downstream the material would disperse outward from the peak at a rate equal to D_L times the concentration gradient in the longitudinal direction. Thus, the peak would flatten and decrease in magnitude as the cloud moves downstream.

Fisher[3] has shown that the dispersion coefficient may be ex-pressed as

$$D_L = \frac{1}{A} \int q'(z) \left[\int_o^z \frac{1}{\Sigma_z \, d(z)} \left(\int_o^z q'(z) \, dz \right) dz \right] dz$$

z is measured laterally across the channel, in which A is the cross sectional area, b the stream width, ε_z the lateral turbulent diffu-sion coefficient, d (z) the flow depth (a function of z) and

$$q'(z) = \int_o^{d(z)} (u-\bar{u}) dy$$

[2] G.I. TAYLOR, "The Dispersion of Matter in Turbulent Flow Through a Pipe", *Proceedings Royal Soc. of London 223A*, 1954, pp. 446-468.
[3] M. B. FISHER, "The Mechanics of Dispersion in Natural Streams", *Journal of the Hydraulics Division*, ASCE, Vol. 93, No. HY 6, Nov. 1967, Proc. Paper 5592, pp. 187-216.

with u the velocity at any point, y, the vertical direction and ū, the mean velocity in the cross-section.

To simplify, a wide rectangular channel will be considered. Using Manning's equation for mean velocity and a commonly accepted empirical relation for ε_z gives

$$D_L = \frac{d^{1/6} b^2 u}{.23\sqrt{g}\; n} \int_o^1 q'(z') \left[\int_o^{z'} \left(\int_o^{z'} q'(z')dz' \right) dz' \right] dz'$$

where $z' = z/b$, n is the Manning roughness coefficient, g the acceleration of gravity, and

$$p'(z') = \frac{u(z')}{\bar{u}} - 1$$

Thus the dispersion coefficient is directly proportional to the mean velocity, to the depth to the one-sixth power, and to the square of the width, and inversely proportional to the roughness. It is also dependent upon the velocity distribution.

The strong dependence upon channel width is shown in published dispersion coefficients for streams in the U.S.[4] Thus, a dispersion coefficient of 90 ft²/sec has been measured on the Green-Duwamish River with a width of 80 feet and one of 2,000 sq.ft/sec has been measured on the Mississippi River with a width of 2,700 feet.

In order to demonstrate the effect of the channel being divided by an island, it is assumed that the transverse velocity distributions are parabolic. If the channel were divided into two equal channels with equal flows, the net result is that the dispersion coefficient is reduced by a factor of two. If it were divided into four equal channels with equal flows the dispersion coefficient would be reduced by four.

The CIP channel past Kettle Island is a more realistic example. Similar parabolic velocity distributions are assumed in both channels. Only about one-sixth of the total flow passes through the CIP channel at low flows. The results of the division of flow into two channels is that the dispersion coefficient is reduced by a factor of 0.53.

    [4] M. K. BONSAL, "Dispersion in Natural Streams", *Journal of the Hydraulic Division*, ASCE, Vol. 97, No. HY11, Nov., 1971, Proc. Paper 8540, p. 1867-1886.

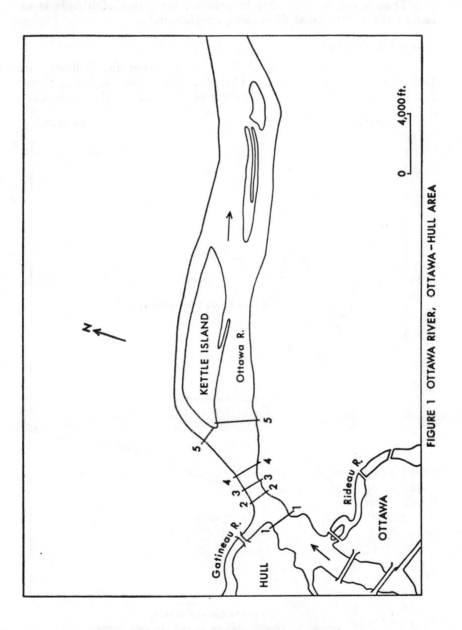

FIGURE 1 OTTAWA RIVER, OTTAWA–HULL AREA

Thus it can be said that in general, the effect of islands is to reduce the longitudinal dispersion coefficient.

ACKNOWLEDGEMENT

This study was financed by a grant from the Ministry of University Affairs, Province of Ontario. The author wishes to thank Dr. Peter Jolly for supplying the air photos used in the analysis.

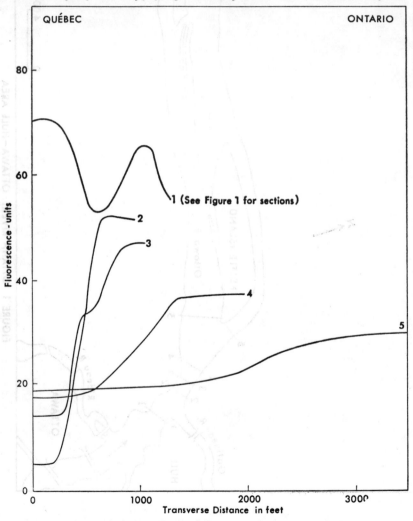

FIGURE 2: FLUORESCENCE IN THE OTTAWA RIVER

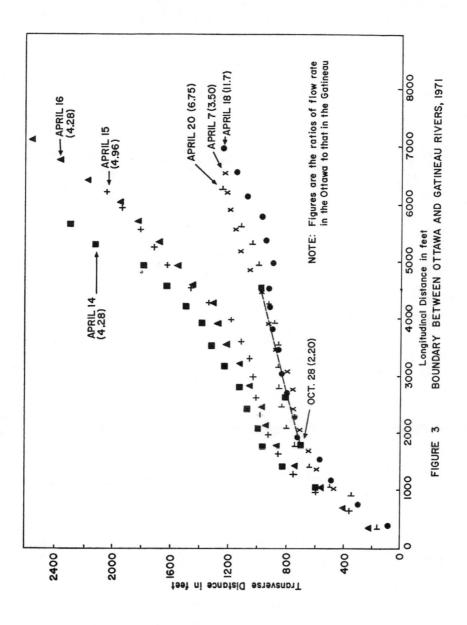

FIGURE 3

BOUNDARY BETWEEN OTTAWA AND GATINEAU RIVERS, 1971

Structures and Processes of Proximal Braided Outwash: Yukon Valley Train and Icelandic Coastal Sandur

B. R. Rust,
Department of Geology,
University of Ottawa

Proximal braided outwash is characterised by coarse heterogeneous bed material in longitudinal bars, which are active only at flood stage. Their morphology is highly variable, but generally comprises a sub-horizontal upper surface, and steeper slopes or cut banks at the downstream lateral margins. The internal structure is poorly-defined sub-horizontal bedding with upstream imbrication of flat pebbles at angles averaging 26°. This structure is consistent with accretion of gravel on the upper surface rather than on forest slopes, as is the case for sand bars in more distal parts of braided systems.

At falling stage channel migration cuts steep banks at downstream lateral margins, until natural revetment by large clasts prevents further erosion. Along sheltered parts of lateral bar margins sand accumulates in wedge-shaped units with internal high-angle cross-stratification overlain by ripple cross-lamination and a mud veneer. Return to flood flow may preserve these wedges if gravel accretes rapidly on the top of the bar. It is thought that gravel is put in motion by flood flow over the cut banks of the previous cycle, a situation which implies upstream bar migration.

Variation in sedimentary facies can be ascribed to proximal-distal and active-stable trends. Both cause an increase in the proportion of fine grained sediment, together with changes in the type and abundance of various sedimentary structures, essentially related to the grain size change. The valley train and coastal sandur types of outwash differ in the areal extent of the facies types, and in the vector properties of the sediment. Directional variance increases downstream in both cases, but more rapidly in coastal plain outwash. The variance of small scale structures is always greater than that of larger structures.

Structure and Process
in a Braided River*

B. R. Rust,
Department of Geology,
University of Ottawa

INTRODUCTION

Much of our present understanding of braiding processes in rivers is based on flume experiments by LEOPOLD and WOLMAN (1957), and on field studies by the same authors, and others such as DOEGLAS (1962) and ORE (1964). SMITH (1970) described prox- imal-distal changes in the Platte Rivers, on which basis the pro-glacial braided rivers of Krigström (1962) and Fahnestock (1963) are proximal, whereas the lower Brahmaputra (COLEMAN, 1969) and the Tana (COLLINSON, 1970) are distal, with relatively fine bed material.

The Donjek is a proximal braided river in the southwest Yukon, Canada, which has been studied from its glacial source downstream for about 80 km (Fig. 1). This work is an extension of the project reported by WILLIAMS and RUST (1969), but with emphasis on the effects of the coarse bedload fraction on braiding processes, and the nature of the structures formed in boulder-rich gravel deposits. An important consideration has been the significance of the study to-wards the understanding of coarse fluvial deposits in the geological record.

HYDROLOGY, MORPHOLOGY, AND BED MATERIAL

Hydrology

Like other proglacial rivers, discharge variation is largely con-trolled by glacial melting, with subsidiary peaks due to summer rain-fall. Unfortunately there are no hydrological records for the Donjek,

* Reproduced from *Sedimentology*, Vol. 18, 1972, pp. 221-245.

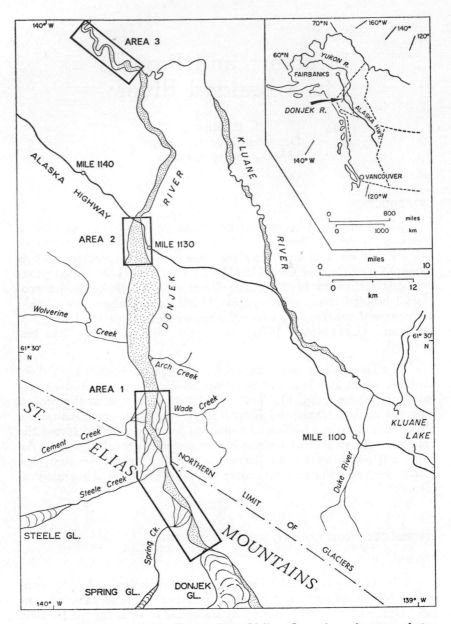

Fig. 1. — Map of part of the Donjek River Valley. Inset shows location relative
to the Yukon River and other parts of northwest North America.

and attempts to measure flood discharge with field equipment were not successful. At the highest stage observed during the 1967 field season, the maximum surface velocity under the bridge at Mile 1,133 on the Alaska Highway was 3.60 m/sec, and the maximum depth was 3.00 m. During studies for bridge construction the Department of Public Works estimated flood discharge at this locality to be about 50,000 ft.^{3}/sec (1,400 m^3/sec), (personal communication, 1968). According to local residents the river continues to flow throughout the winter, with discharge greatly reduced, and sediment load almost eliminated.

The Slims is another proglacial river located about 45 km east of the Donjek, which flows into Kluane Lake, and is therefore an indirect tributary to the Donjek. FAHNESTOCK (1970) estimated its maximum discharge at about 20,000 ft.^{3}/sec (570 m^3/sec), which suggests that the figure of 50,000 ft.^{3}/sec is of the right order for the Donjek. Records of discharge in the Kluane River at the lake outlet have been kept by the Water Survey of Canada since 1953, and show that the peak generally occurs in mid-August, and averaged 9,350 ft.^{3}/sec (265 m^3/sec) over the recorded period.

River morphology

The Donjek valley was formed by Pleistocene glacial erosion, followed by subsequent retreat of the glaciers, with occasional re-advances (MULLER, 1967). Down valley from the glacial end moraines, fluvial deposits now cover the valley floor, which can be divided into active, non-vegetated tracts, which are generally flooded each year, and relatively stable vegetated areas, commonly separated by erosional banks (Fig. 2). The stabilized areas are higher than the active tracts, and can be approximately dated by the nature and density of the vegetation present (WILLIAMS and RUST, 1969).

Like most large braided rivers, a single dominant channel can generally be distinguished within the overall braided pattern, although in some sections there are several principal channels. The channel patterns represented are typified by the three study areas of Fig. 1 and 2. In downstream order they comprise Area 1, with a zig-zag channel pattern; Area 2, a straight braided reach; and a meandering reach with internal braids (Area 3). In order to characterize these patterns, channel sinuosities and total braiding indices (BRICE, 1964) were measured in each area (Table I). However, measurement of the braiding index is dependent on the definition of the bar margin, which varies with river stage. The index tends to convey a false

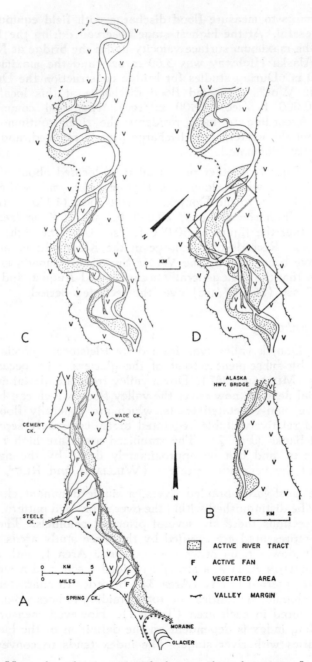

Fig. 2. — Maps of reaches investigated, showing channel patterns. In most cases
the active and vegetated areas are separated by erosional banks. A.
Area 1; B. Area 2; C. Area 3, 1956-57; D. Area 3, 1970. The areas
enclosed within double lines are shown enlarged in Fig. 11.

impression of numerical accuracy, which could in some cases be assessed more meaningfully by visual inspection, as low, moderate or high degrees of braiding. In the Donjek, Areas 1 and 2 are characterized by a high degree of braiding, whereas Area 3 is a meandering reach, with moderate internal braiding.

TABLE 1

Average Channel Parameters

Study area	Slope	Sinuosity				Total braiding index	N
		active	N	stable	N		
Tributary fans							
Arch Creek	0.04[1]						
Cement Creek	0.025						
Spring Creek	0.019						
Steele Creek	0.013						
Donjek River							
Area 1	0.006[1]	1.17	64	1.15	40	14.0	4
Area 2	0.0006[1]	1.07[2]	6	1.09[2]	6	2.2[2]	
Area 3	0.00085[1]						
Main channel		1.74				2.94	3
Minor channels		1.08	8				

Total braiding index: $2 \times$ sum of lengths of bars and islands in reach/length of reach (Brice, 1964).
N = number of observations.
[1] Determined photogrammetrically on water surface in the middle of the main channel; [2] data from Williams and Rust (1969, table 2).

In Area 1 the main channel is fairly distinct, and has a zig-zag pattern due to the presence of alluvial fans at the mouths of steep, narrow canyons, which carry tributary creeks into the river. The larger creeks are active enough to divert the river from a straight down-valley course, being fed by meltwater from their own valley glaciers, or receiving water from small hanging glaciers. They go through a seasonal hydrological cycle similar to that of the Donjek, but the increase in runoff in the Spring is more rapid on account of the higher slopes of the fans, the creeks, and their drainage areas. The slopes on individual fans are quite constant, and increase with decreasing size from 0.04 for Arch Creek, the smallest fan investigated, to 0.013 for Steele Creek fan, the largest in the area. In contrast, the average slope of the Donjek in Area 1 is 0.006.

The boundaries between the fans and the river are approximately linear and not arcuate, as would be expected from the intersection of a cone and a planar surface. The linear boundaries are present where the river abuts inactive parts of a fan, and probably reflect the ability of the river to revert to a straight reach in the absence of fan activity. The result is that the fan areas are trimmed to an approximately rhombic shape, with the active fan apex at the outer corner of the rhombus (Fig. 2A). This causes constrictions in the river opposite fan apices, an effect noted by FAHNESTOCK (1970, p. 164) in the Slims River.

The sinuosities of channels in Area 1 were measured on air photographs divided into sections normal to flow direction, and separated into active and stable parts within each section. The results (Table I) reveal no significant difference betwen the sinuosities of channels in the active and stable parts. This shows that there is no change in shape as channels are filled during stabilisation, and that the sinuosity of channels in ancient rocks is likely to be the same as that of channels in the original active area.

Downstream from Area 1 the river valley is wider, and the surrounding country is much lower. The slope and sediment transport capabilities of the tributaries are therefore greatly reduced, and the river develops into an essentially straight reach with a braided pattern. This section extends from the downstream end of Area 1 to the upstream end of Area 3, and is typified by Area 2 (Fig. 2B). The average slope within this reach is 0.0006; other channel parameters are given in Table I, and the area was described in some detail by WILLIAMS and RUST (1969).

Below its confluence with the Kluane River the Donjek enters a reach in which the main channel is more distinct, and has a meandering pattern (Fig. 2C) with an average sinuosity of 1.74 and average slope 0.00085. The increased slope is unexpected in view of the channel pattern relationship established by LEOPOLD and WOLMAN (1957), who defined a meandering channel as one with a sinuosity of 1.5 or greater. They showed that the development of braided as opposed to meandering channels was related to greater discharge and slope values, which fall above the line $S = 0.06Q^{-0.44}$, where S is the slope and Q is the discharge in ft.³/sec.

The Kluane differs from the other local rivers in having a much smaller sediment load, and a discharge that fluctuates less markedly, being controlled by the level of Kluane Lake rather than by glacial melting. It may therefore induce the anomalous change in the Donjek's channel pattern by diluting its load and damping the seasonal fluctuation in discharge. An additional factor is that the river valley is narrower in the lower part of the straight reach, between the Alaska Highway bridge and the upstream end of Area 3. FAHNESTOCK (1970) observed that narrower tracts of the Slims River have lower slopes than broader reaches, an effect also present in the Rio Grande (HARMS and FAHNESTOCK 1965, p. 87).

The main channel in Area 3 also has islands and bars, and with a total braiding index of 2.94 can be described as a meandering reach with moderate internal braiding. Minor channels elsewhere in Area 3 show the braided pattern more clearly, and have an average sinuosity of 1.08. Area 3 is the only part of the river in which major changes of the principal channels and erosion of previously stable banks and islands have occurred since the last air photos were taken in 1956 and 1957 (Fig. 2C, D). This suggests that the meandering reach is in a state of disequilibrium, but the sinuosities of old channels on vegetated areas that are at least a century old appear to be much the same as those of present channels.

Bed material

Glacial deposits (chiefly morainic) furnish almost the entire sedimentary source for the Donjek and its tributaries, except for the Kluane River. Isolated mounds of partially reworked moraine persist for about 8 km below the terminus of the Donjek Glacier, and glacial sediments are probably present at shallow depth throughout the reaches studied. The river banks are composed of moraine material reworked to varying degrees by fluvial action, with small sections of bed-rock, loess and peat.

Size analyses of the finer sediments and matrix samples from the coarse sediments were performed by sieving of the pebble fraction and by sedimentation of the sand and mud fractions. The approximate size distribution of fragments too large to be included in matrix samples was determined by making point counts on photographs of fresh exposures taken at the sampling site, and converted to volume distribution.

The grain size parameters of the finer-grained sediments are not significantly different from those given by WILLIAMS and RUST (1969, fig. 4, 7; appendix 1). The results for the coarse sediments

(Fig. 3A) show the wide range of particle sizes in the source and
bed material of the river. The winnowing effect of fluvial processes
is evident from the grain size differentiation between till and river
gravel (Fig. 3B). The mean and maximum grain sizes of bed material both decrease downstream, due to the progressive inability of
the river to move the larger particles as slope decreases; changes in
maximum grain size are shown in Fig. 13B, p. 118. Measurements
of mean size were not attempted, but changes are obvious from the
increase in fines relative to gravel in the downstream direction. This
trend can be seen on low altitude air photos, but exposed sections
generally show that the proportion of gravel increases below the
surface. For this reason, the surface sampling method of WOLMAN
(1954) could not be used.

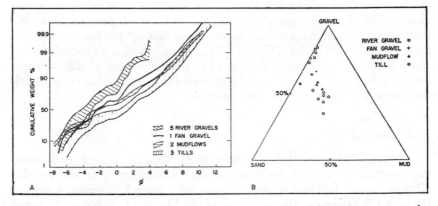

Fig. 3. — Grain-size characteristics of source material and Donjek river gravels.
A. Grain size curves; B. Triangular gravel-sand-mud diagram.

FACIES

The facies classification used in this paper is slightly simplified
from that of WILLIAMS and RUST (1969), which was partly aimed
at distinguishing facies types common in stable parts of Area 2, but
less abundant in the river as a whole. The revised classification is
described below, with letters in brackets referring to the earlier
nomenclature.

Facies 1: silt and clay (A and B, the latter more varied in lithology)

This facies is made up of parallel-laminated silt and clay,
deposited from stagnant water in channels cut off as water level

Fig. 4. — A sand wedge deposited at the lateral margin of a gravel bar at falling stage has been later dissected by water in minor channels draining off the bar. The water in the main channel is now stagnant, and is depositing a thin film of mud on underlying ripples.

falls. In active reaches this results in the formation of a thin film of mud covering structures formed at higher stage (Fig. 4), but judging from the rarity of this material in vertical sections, its preservation potential is low. Thicker, preservable deposits of parallel-laminated sediment accumulate in older, stable tracts, where vegetation has a binding effect on the mud, and each lamina represents the suspended load from one flood cycle. This facies gives rise to the best preservation of animal trails, plant remains (apart from logs), rain prints, and desiccation cracks.

Facies 2: cross-stratified sand (D)

This facies comprises cross-stratal sets which are mostly tabular, although some have trough-shaped lower bounding surfaces. The latter shape is due to deposition in smaller channels or scour hollows, and appears to be independent of the mode of formation of the cross-strata. The sets are commonly between 30 and 90 cm thick, with dips between 20 and 30° (occasionally less, especially where gravel layers are present). The cross-strata are locally planar, although their three-dimensional form is somewhat sinuous when traced later-ally for any distance. This facies is formed by the migration of transverse bars (ORE, 1964) in isolated active channels on stable areas, or in sheltered parts of active tracts. Bars of this type are rare in the Donjek.

Facies 3: ripple-laminated silty sand (C_1)

Sets of cross-laminated silty sand show a size range in accord-ance with the migrating ripples that form them, having an average thickness of 2.5 cm. They vary from erosionally-bound through-shaped sets to ripple-drift sets with preserved lee-side and stoss-side laminae, and commonly include plant fragments. These features indicate considerable variation in flow conditions during ripple mig-ration. Facies 3 is commonly present on the upper bounding surfaces of cross-bed sets (facies 2), but also develops independently in minor channels on bar surfaces.

The ripples themselves are abundant and variable (WILLIAMS and Rust 1969, pp. 654-655), and show many instances of associa-tion between primary current-formed and secondary wave-generated types. They are similar to structures described as interference ripples by PICARD and HIGH (1970), but the terms primary and secondary are used here because the wave ripples are consequent upon rather than interfering with current action. The secondary ripples are com-monly, but not always symmetrical in profile, and are formed in several ways. The examples shown in Fig. 5 were produced by lateral waves generated at the margin of a channel by pulsation of the primary stream flow. Their axes are generally normal to those of the current ripples, but they are diffracted around emergent objects such as pebbles and primary ripple crests. In other cases diffraction gives rise to true patterns of interference between two sets of secondary ripples. Fig. 5 also shows a transition from ripples to current crescents with the change in bed lithology from sand to sand-and-pebbles (lower left upper right).

In other examples the secondary ripples are formed by wind action on the water held only in the primary ripple troughs, after a

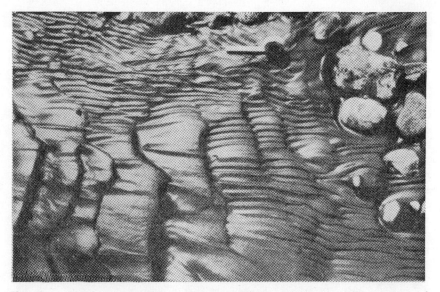

Fig. 5. — Primary asymmetric ripples formed by current flowing left to right, and secondary symmetric ripples formed by lateral waves generated at the channel margin. The secondary ripples increase in abundance towards the channel margin (top of photograph); ripples are transitional into current crescents where pebbles emerge (top right corner).

fall in water level (Fig. 6). Several small terraces eroded by waves at successive water levels can also be seen.

Facies 4: "quick" silty sand (C_2)

This facies is present in sheltered parts of active tracts. It lacks internal structure, and is characterized by flowing readily when loaded, a property related to conditions of water saturation and size distribution, which have not been investigated. The facies is absent from stable areas, probably because of dehydration, and from Area 1 because of the lack of thick silty sand accumulations.

Facies 5: wind-blown deposits (E)

Although not strictly correct, it is convenient to define a facies on the basis of eolian transportation and deposition. On account of its coarse bedload, the Donjek is less subject to these processes than rivers with finer beds, such as the Slims (FAHNESTOCK, 1970).

Wind-formed dunes are not present; the sand is deposited in low-amplitudes ripples, and most of the wind-blown silt forms scattered loess deposits in the surrounding forests.

A structure formed by deposition of wind-blown fine sand on a damp surface is illustrated in Fig 7; similar structures are formed by the action of wind on snow (CORNISH, 1914). In the present case, dry grains transported by the wind stick to the damp surface of the sediment, which contains sufficient moisture to wet the newly-arrived grains by capillary action. More grains can then be trapped, and the ground surface builds up into the wind at a low angle to produce structures with steep (in some cases overhanging) stoss-sides and gently sloping lee-sides. In examples described by VAN STRAATEN (1953, p. 42) the stoss-sides are regularly spaced at right angles to the wind, and he termed them anti-ripplets, because their asymmetry with respect to wind direction is the reverse of normal ripples. REINECK (1955) called similar structures "Haftrippeln", and

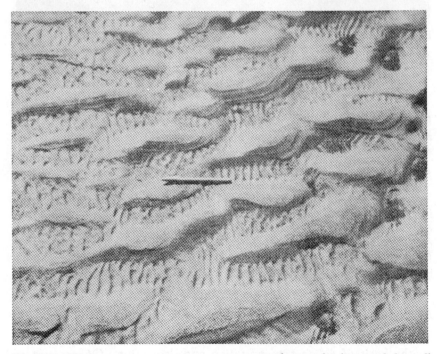

Fig. 6. — Wind action on water in primary ripple troughs has eroded small terraces and generated secondary ripples oriented perpendicular to the primary ripples.

Fig. 7. — Structures formed by deposition of wind-blown fine sand on a damp
surface. Wind direction from top to bottom of photograph.

others with an irregular form "Haftwarzen", but neither term can
be readily translated into English. The examples shown in Fig. 7
have their strongest and most regular component parallel to the wind
direction, with a radiating plumose structure towards the margins of
each "ripple". This structure reflects the mode of growth, and is
probably related to the directions in which the rising capillary water
moves.

*Facies 6: gravel, with minor sand and mud accretions (G and F, the
latter more variable in lithology)*

This facies or facies complex is formed by the migration of
bars in which gravel is the major component. The gravel is either
structureless, or is disposed in poorly defined horizontal beds (maximum dip 3°). The nature of the surfaces beneath sets of horizontal
beds was not determined, because of the poor definition and the
difficulty of excavating coarse gravel, but they are probably low
angle erosional contacts. SMITH (1970) refers to a similar structure
in gravel bars of the Platte Rivers as horizontal stratification, and
discusses it together with horizontal stratification in sand, a type of

bedding formed under somewhat different conditions. In order to distinguish the two features, and at the same time reflect differences in stratal thickness, the terms lamination and bedding are restricted in this paper to horizontal stratification in sand and gravel respectively.

The gravel bars are termed longitudinal[1], on account of their elongation parallel to the local flow direction, with an average length/width ratio of 3.9, and lengths varying between 150 and 450 m. Plan shape varies greatly from a characteristic elongate rhombic form, pointed at both ends. The bars are generally asymetric both parallel and normal to the flow direction, with asymmetry normal to flow consisting of a ridge parallel to the bar axis, but nearer to one side. The main channels are also commonly asymmetric, and in the same sense as the bars, so that their gently sloping margins grade into the adjacent gentle bar slopes, and the steep surfaces are correspondingly related. In most cases, however, the gradation between channel and bar is interrupted along part of the bar margin by the development of erosional banks. These banks are steep (Fig. 8, 9), and in some cases are partly vertical, but they appear to be stable at water levels below that of flood stage (p. 121). During the period 6-23 June, 1970, none of the observed banks retreated, except for one located opposite the point where Spring Creek enters the Donjek. In flood the creek directed very rapid flows against this bank, and caused an average retreat of 3 m. in less than a week.

Bar asymmetry parallel to flow generally takes the form of a gently sloping upstream surface which grades into shallow water above the bar, and a steeper downstream (partly lateral) slope which merges with the steeper bank of the adjacent channel (Fig. 8). The topography of the bar surface is commonly complicated by minor channels, scours, log accumulations, and beach ridges. Scours are generally elongate parallel to the local flow direction, and are formed at the intersection of minor channels, or below logs, when they take the form of large current crescents. Beach ridges are sand accumulations formed at the lateral margins of longitudinal bars in areas protected from the main current, for example downstream of prominent corners in the bar margin. The ridges are straight or gently curved,

---

[1] More distal braided rivers are characterized by transverse sand bars (Ore, 1964) or linguoid bars (Collinson, 1970). Transverse crescentic gravel bars were reported from the North Saskatchewan River (Galay and Neill, 1967), but have not been observed in the Donjek. Braid bar (Allen 1968, p. 38) may be used as a general term for any type of bar responsible for a braided pattern.

and are symmetric, with planar surfaces sloping at low angles on each side (COLLINSON, 1970, fig. 14), commonly lineated down dip. The ridges form at the breaking point of waves generated by the primary current flow. Wave swash carries sand up the ridge to

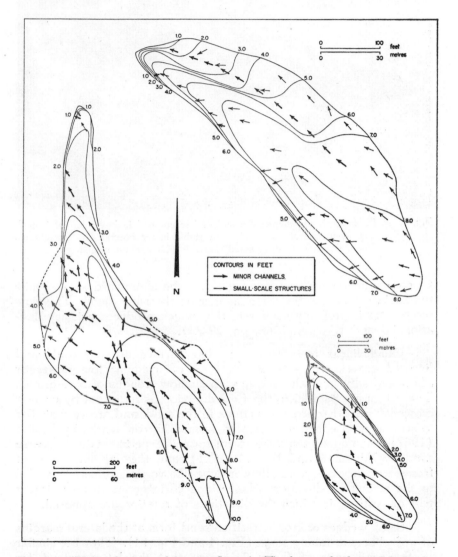

Fig. 8. — Maps of surveyed bars in Area 1. The bar in the lower left is also shown in Fig. 9.

Fig. 9. — Photograph of downstream end of bar mapped in lower left of Fig. 8. The steep lateral banks (*B*) are stable under normal flow conditions, but in flood short steep-sided channels (*C*) are cut into them.

its crest, and thence transports it down the shoreward slope, while the backwash acts in the same manner on the outer slope. The flow mechanism is probably similar to that which produces primary linea-tion in sand (ALLEN, 1968, pp. 29-33).

Other linear features on the bar surface are log trails and lineated gravel, which takes the form of irregular low ridges or ribbons of silty sand alternating with shallow troughs of bare gravel. The ridges are parallel to the flow direction as indicated by current crescents and other scour structures in the sand, and are very similar to structures in ephemeral streams, termed harrow marks by KARCZ (1967). Analogous structures were formed experimentally in coarse sand by WOLMAN and BRUSH (1961), and they appear to result from secondary transverse flow in tube-like vortices oriented parallel to the main flow direction. Each ridge corresponds to an adjacent pair of vortices, in which the directions of rotation are opposed.

Small wedges of cross-stratified sand form at the lateral margins of gravel bars at falling stage (Fig. 4 and Fig. 14). They are similar to the sand units of facies 2, except that the latter extend for hundreds of meters (the order of bar length) in the cross-stratal dip direction. In contrast, the sand wedges extend for only a few meters, and they are therefore included within the gravel facies. Also included are small accumulations of ripple-laminated sand, horizontally-laminated sand, and mud veneers, (in order of decreasing preservation potential).

In some cases horizontal lamination can be related to a smooth surface topography, for example Fig. 10, which shows a gravel ridge oriented perpendicular to current flow (towards the camera), as indicated by ripples above and below the ridge. The upstream and downstream slopes of the ridge are covered with plane beds of fine sand, showing distinct lineation parallel to the flow direction. These changes in bed-form from ripples to plane bed to ripples are due to transition from lower to upper to lower flow regimes in response to shallowing of water over the ridge. Lineation does not continue over the crest of the ridge because the transport rate was too high to allow the deposition of fine sediment.

Fig. 10. — A gravel ridge oriented normal to current flow (towards camera, parallel to shovel) shows variation in bed-forms related to change in depth of flow. Lineated flat sand-beds like those immediately upstream and downstream of the gravel ridge are rarely preserved in the Donjek.

DIRECTIONAL PROPERTIES

In Area 2 WILLIAMS and RUST (1969, fig. 26, p. 675) measured
the current directions of populations of small-scale structures (mostly
ripples), and the range of channel orientations. Both sets of data
gave reasonable approximations of the river trend, although the bisector of the extremes of channel orientation was closer (5°W) than
the vector mean of the small-scale structures (22°W). COLEMAN
(1969) measured the orientation of cross-strata in sand bars of the
Brahmaputra River, and discovered a comparable directional correspondence between the minor structures and the river trend.

Similar observations were made on Area 3 on the Donjek to
determine the effect of a meandering main channel on the minor
directional features. Data analysis by the method of CURRAY (1956)
shows a close approximation between the local vector means of small-
scale structures and local channel orientation (Fig. 11). The grand
vector mean for all small-scale structures (2,550 observations) is 11°
clockwise from the river trend, whereas the vector mean of 113
random channel orientations is 5° anticlockwise of the river trend
(Fig. 12; Tables II, III). Compared with the data for Area 2, this
result indicates that the correspondence between the mean vectors
and the river trend is equally good in the two areas. However, the
meandering channel pattern does have an effect on the vector magnitudes, which are lower in Area 3, indicating greater directional
variance in the meandering reach.

In view of the results from Areas 2 and 3 it was concluded that
the correspondence between the vector properties of small-scale
structures and channels had been adequately demonstrated. Accordingly, and because gravel is markedly dominant over sand in Area 1,
the orientation of pebbles was measured instead of ripple populations.
In each case pebbles were measured within a channel, so that their
orientation could be compared with a known current direction. The
results show that for rod-shaped pebbles there is a strong long-axis
preferred orientation perpendicular to current flow, and for platy
pebbles there is a distinct upstream imbrication. In the case of
elongate pebbles the degree of preferred orientation is greater for
a mixed sand and pebble bed, whereas imbrication of flat pebbles
is better developed on a purely pebble bed. These data will be
discussed in more detail elsewhere (RUST, 1972).

Channel orientations in Area 1 were treated in a slightly different way from that used for Areas 2 and 3. Three enlarged aerial
photographs, each with a different river trend, were divided into

sub-areas, and the range of channel arcs within sub-areas was determined, as well as the total range of channel orientation for the whole photograph. The results (Tables II, III) show that on average the channel arc bisector approximates the river trend within about 2°, whichever way it is worked out. In addition, a square grid was placed over each photograph, and the orientation of the channel nearest to each intersection was measured, averaged for each sub-area, and then for the whole photograph. This method gave vector means which were on average about 5° from the river trend, and high vector magnitudes. The latter procedure is considered to approximate most closely the conditions imposed by ancient rock outcrops, and therefore has the most significance for paleocurrent studies.

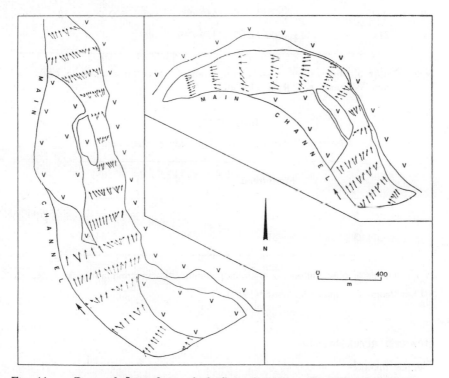

Fig. 11. — Parts of Area 3 in which flow directions of small-scale structures were measured. Each arrow is a local vector mean calculated from ten observations.

TABLE II

Directional Properties — Channels

Area Photo		River trend	Section of photo	Random channel orientation			Channel arcs				
Area	Photo			N	$\overline{\chi}$	L	total maximum range	arc bisector	average maximum range	N	arc bisector
1	I	004	IA	96	009	92.4	303–071	007	315.6–057.6	19	007
			IB	89	007	90.2	291–074	003			
	II	343		139	352	84.4	265–061	343	298–042	14	350
	III	000	IIIA	100	006	90.2	276–089	002	306–052	10	359
			IIIB	89	004	81.6	297–073	005	312–049	9	000
2[1]		000					260–090	355	300–060	12	001
3		311		113	306	62.6	179–049	294			

N = number of observations $\overline{\chi}$ = vector mean; L = vector magnitude (%).
[1] Data from Williams and Rust (1969).

TABLE III

Directional Properties — Small-Scale Structures

	River trend	N	$\overline{\chi}$	L
2[1]	000	660	338	
3	311	2550	322	84.31

N = number of observations; $\overline{\chi}$ = vector mean; L = vector magnitude (%).
[1] Data from Williams and Rust (1969).

BRAIDED RIVER MODEL

Facies model

A facies model for the Donjek can be constructed from the geographical variation in abundance of the facies types already described. On this basis two major trends emerge, a proximal-distal trend, and an active-stable trend. Thus the abundances of facies 1, 2, 3, 4 and 5 increase downstream, while that of facies 6 decreases. Facies 1 is more abundant on stable areas, where vegetation is established and flood flow is uncommon. These relationships are summarized in Fig. 13.

The model can be applied to braided rivers in general by extending the variation trends beyond the limits found in the Donjek.

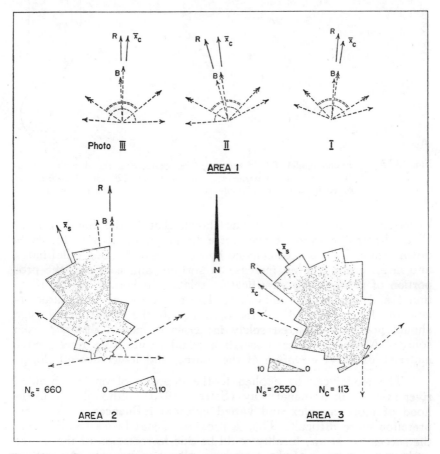

Fig. 12. — Summary diagram of directional data from Areas 1, 2, and 3. Data for Area 2 from Williams and Rust (1969, fig. 26).

R = river trend; χ_s = vector mean of small-scale structures; χ_c = vector mean of channel orientations; B = channel arc bisector.

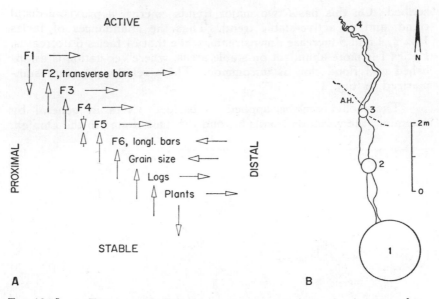

Fig. 13. A. — Facies model. *F1* = facies 1; arrows indicate the direction of increase of a given parameter. See text (pp. 229-236) for definition of each facies. B. Change in maximum grain size downriver.

For example, SMITH (1970) has shown that in the South Platte-Platte River the ratio of transverse to longitudinal bars increases downstream. This is accompanied by decrease of the bed-relief index and mean grain size, an increase in sorting, and a rise in the proportion of planar cross-stratification relative to horizontal stratification (sand and gravel combined). These changes are all characteristic of the proximal-distal trend, although the distal facies type should not be considered solely in terms of actual distance from source. A similar facies association could result from finer source material, or lower elevation of the source, and lower overall slopes.

The model can be applied to the deposits of ancient braided river systems in a similar way (SMITH, 1970), although the likelihood of more complex and varied external influences make interpretation more difficult. Thus a proximal-distal facies trend within the succession at any locality could be due to recession of the source with time, lowering of the source, or climatic changes. An active-stable trend within the succession could be related to the same external environmental changes, but in most cases a more likely explanation would be diversion of the active river tract away from the locality in question. A stable-active facies trend is explicable by a reverse of the changes described above.

Vector model

ALLEN (1966) has shown that vector models for fluid flow systems can be constructed from theoretical considerations, but that current structures of different orders of magnitude may contribute different vectors within a given flow system. This conclusion can also be applied to models developed from observations on rivers, and has considerable value in paleogeographical studies.

In the Donjek, longitudinal bars and channels have the expected unimodal distribution about the river trend. However, in terms of paleogeography the preservation of complete bars is most unlikely, and the measurement of channel orientation requires very good exposure. The only directional property likely to be commonly preserved and observable in sediments of ancient gravel bars is the

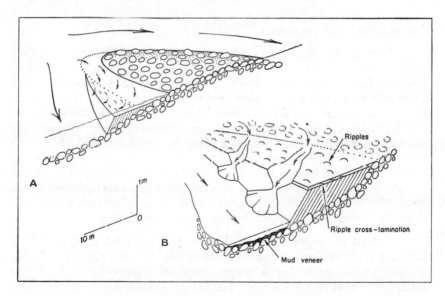

Fig. 14. A. — Formation of a sand wedge lateral to a gravel bar. Planar cross-strata form by outward migration of a slip face, while ripples migrate across the topset surface to form ripple cross-lamination. B. Dissection of sand wedges after further fall in stage to the point at which mud starts to settle from suspension on the channel bed (cf. Fig. 4). Scale is approximate.

preferred orientation of platy or elongate clasts. In the present study both kinds of modal orientation have been shown to relate closely to the local channel trends. A unimodal distribution about the river trend would therefore be expected, but each vector requires a large number of observations, and the method is very tedious.

High-angle cross-stratification and ripple cross-lamination in sand have the highest potential for preservation and recognition in ancient fluvial sediments. The vector properties of both types of structure are related to bar orientation, but they would be expected to have higher variances on account of flow divergence during their depositional stages (Fig. 14). This has been demonstrated with respect to ripple orientation, which gives a unimodal distribution with a vector mean close to the river trend, but a greater variance than channel orientation (Fig. 12). The orientation of cross-stratified sand bodies was not investigated, but it is possible that they would give a bimodal distribution, on account of their tendency to form at lateral bar margins.

Longitudinal bar migration

From the results of experiments LEOPOLD and WOLMAN (1957) suggested that longitudinal bars are initiated by deposition of coarser bedload fractions in the middle of a channel. Subsequent growth takes place by addition of finer sediment on top of and downstream of the bar nucleus, until it is raised above water level. Observations by the same authors indicated that a similar process, followed by vegetative stabilisation, may take place in small braided rivers. In the Donjek, however, bar stabilisation does not appear to operate on an individual basis. Instead, whole areas become stable as the active part of the river tract is diverted elsewhere; channels are gradually filled with finer sediment, and plant colonisation proceeds through a series of changes to the climax vegetation.

Braided rivers with relatively fine bed material tend to follow Leopold and Wolman's model. COLEMAN (1969) reported downstream migration during a single flood of nearly 5,000 ft. for a relatively small sand bar in the lower Brahmaputra River. Bar migration took place by addition of sediment to the more gentle downstream slopes of the bars, with equivalent erosion at the steeper upstream margins. CHIEN (1961) observed bar movements of 90-120 m/day in the lower Yellow River, a large braided stream with median grain size in the silt range. It is notable that in the Brahmaputra the longitudinal asymmetry of bars is the reverse of that in the Donjek, and it is unlikely that close comparisons would be valid between rivers with such different bed materials.

The question remains as to whether the sequence of events described by LEOPOLD and WOLMAN (1957) is applicable to braided rivers with coarse bedloads, and what is the significance of variation in slope. FAHNESTOCK (1963) observed very rapid minor changes in the channel pattern of the White River, a glacial outwash stream on Mount Rainier, Washington. The rapidity of change is probably related to the high slope (0.01-0.08) of the reaches studied. Similar rapid and unpredictable changes of bar and channel configuration take place on a small tributary fan which joins the Donjek River between Spring Creek and the glacier terminus. The slope of this fan is within the range quoted for the White River, and is probably the most important cause of rapid bar movement.

In rivers like the Donjek, the high proportion of coarse bed material (Fig. 3) and the lower slope combine to make the bars essentially immobile, except during peak flood. The intensity of flood required to cause significant bar migration, and the periodicity and duration of such an event are not known at present. Bar migration cannot be observed directly, because of the highly turbid water during flood. Similar problems were no doubt inherent in KRIGSTRÖM's (1962) studies of glacial outwash streams in Iceland, which appear to be more like the Donjek than others recorded in the literature, although Krigström does not give figures for slope or size of bed material.

In the present study these problems are approached in two ways: (1) investigation of bed-forms and internal structures of the bars; and (2) long-term observation of bar and bed-load movement. Several longitudinal bars have been mapped in detail, including directional structures such as minor channels and ripple populations (Fig. 8). The generalised contours show the basic bar morphology: relatively gentle slopes at the upstream end, and steep slopes at downstream lateral banks. Short, steep-sided channels cutting through these banks are the most evident sites of erosion on the bars (Fig. 9). If Leopold and Wolman's model is applicable to rivers with coarse bed-loads, the gravel beds formed by bar migration should dip downstream at steeper angles than the water surface, although considerable directional variation would be expected on account of variable orientation of the bar and its downstream margins. The attitude of gravel beds in the Donjek varies about the horizontal, with dips up to about 3° both upstream and downstream, suggesting that the flatter upstream bar surface is the preferred site of deposition. If this is so, it follows that the main sites of gravel erosion are the steep downstream slopes of bars further up-river, and that bars migrate upstream. Horizontal bedding also implies transportation of gravel in planar sheets, a condition which would be expected in the very high energy flow required to move such coarse material.

As the flood subsides, the gravel gradually stops moving, and flow over the bar diverges from its emergent axis. This process concentrates flow in the channels, which for a short time many migrate laterally and cut steep erosional banks, usually located towards the downstream end of the bar. These banks soon become stable, because large boulders falling to the foot of the bank cannot be moved as the current slackens, and act as protection against further erosion. The result is that steep high banks persist until the next flood, when they become the site of very rapid erosion as water sweeps over them from the bar. Continued fall in the water level causes greater lateral divergence of flow, and sand begins to accumulate in wedges at the bar margins, which build outwards to form sets of high-angle cross-strata (Fig. 14A). Ripples migrate across the top of the sand wedges to deposit sets of ripple cross-lamination, until further fall in the water level causes dissection of the sand body (Fig. 4, 14B). The water now flows over the bar surface in isolated channels, and cuts V-shaped canyons across the sand wedges, depositing the eroded sand as small deltas at the channel margin. The last stage of the cycle occurs when the water in the channel stagnates, and the suspended silt and clay settle to form a thin film on the bed. In more active channels this last stage occurs rarely or never.

The present observations are not sufficient to prove or disprove the flood cycle described above, but it is hoped that long-term investigations will do so. These take the form of low-level air photography, and monitoring of painted pebbles and boulders on bars. At several sites on each surveyed bar a number of rocks was measured and painted, with as far as possible an even distribution up to the largest size present. Over a period of years some of the rocks eroded from a given site should be traceable, while those remaining can be easily monitored. The largest boulders will be removed only by exceptional flood conditions, and can be used in the interim as fixed points for aerial photography and mapping.

ACKNOWLEDGEMENTS

I would like to thank Professors D. L. Dineley and P. Allen for generous provision of facilities at the Universities of Bristol and Reading; Jeff Smith, Ken Lowndes, and Dr. Peter Johnson for field assistance; and the Arctic Institute of North America for logistic support, particularly flying services by Phil Upton. Thanks are also due to Drs. J. R. L. Allen and H. G. Reading for comments on the manuscript; to Surveys and Mapping Branch, Ottawa, Ont., for photogrammetric services; and to the National Research Council of Canada for financial support.

REFERENCES

ALLEN, J. R. L., (1966), "On Bedforms and Palaeocurrents", *Sedimentology,* 6:153-190.

— (1968), *Current Ripples,* Amsterdam, North-Holland, 433 p.

BRICE, J. C., (1964), "Channel Patterns and Terraces of the Loup Rivers in Nebraska", *U.S. Geol. Surv., Prof. Pap.,* 422-D:1-41.

CHIEN, N., (1961), "The Braided Stream of the Lower Yellow River", *Sci. Sin. (Peking),* 10:734-754.

COLEMAN, J. M., (1969), "Brahmaputra River: Channel Process and Sedimentation", *Sediment. Geol.,* 3:129-239.

COLLINSON, J. D., (1970), "Bedforms of the Tana River, Norway", *Geogr. Ann.,* 52:31-56.

CORNISH, V., (1914), *Waves of Sand and Snow and the Eddies which Make Them,* London, Fisher Unwin, 383 pp.

CURRAY, J. R., (1956), "The Analysis of Two-dimensional orientation Data", *J. Geol.,* 64:117-131.

DOEGLAS, D. J., (1962), "The Structure and Sedimentary deposits of Braided Rivers", *Sedimentology,* 1:167-190.

FAHNESTOCK, R. K., (1963), "Morphology and Hydrology of a Glacial Stream — White River, Mt. Rainier, Washington", *U.S. Geol. Surv., Prof. Pap.,* 422-A:1-70.

— (1970), "Morphology of the Slims River", in: V. C. BUSHNELL and R. H. RAGLE (Editors), *Scientific Results, Icefield Ranges Research Project. Am. Geogr. Soc. — Arct. Inst., N. Am.,* 1:161-172.

GALAY, V. J. and NEILL, C. R., (1967), "Discussion on "Nomenclature for Bed Forms in Alluvial Channels", *Proc. Am. Assoc. Civ. Eng., J. Hydraul. Div.,* 93:130-133.

HARMS, J. C., and FAHNESTOCK, R. K., (1965), "Stratification, Bedforms, and Flow Phenomena (with an example from the Rio Grande)", in: G. V. MIDDLETON (Editor), *Primary Sedimentary Structures and their Hydrodynamic Interpretation* — *Soc. Econ. Paleontol. Mineral., Spec. Publ.,* 12:84-115.

KARCZ, I., (1967), Harrow Marks, Current-aligned Sedimentary Structures", *J. Geol.,* 75:113-121.

KRIGSTRÖM, A., (1962), "Geomorphological Studies of Sandur Plains and their Braided Rivers in Iceland", *Geogr. Ann.,* 44:328-346.

LEOPOLD, L. B., and WOLMAN, M. G., (1957), "River Channel Patterns: Straight, meandering, and Braided", *U.S. Geol. Surv., Prof. Pap.,* 282-B:39-85.

MULLER, J. E., (1967), Kluane Lake Map-area, Yukon Territory (115G, 115E, E½)", *Geol. Surv. Can., Mem.* 340, 137 pp.

ORE, H. T., (1964), "Some Criteria for Recognition of Braided Stream Deposits", *Univ. Wyo. Contrib. Geol.,* 3:1-14.

PICARD, M. D., and HIGH, L. R., (1970), "Interference Ripple Marks formed by Ephemeral Streams", *J. Sediment. Petrol.,* 40:708-711.

REINECK, H.-E., (1965), "Haftrippeln und Haftwarzen, Ablagerungsformen von Flugsand", *Senckend. Lethaea,* 36:347-357.

RUST, B. R., (1972), "Pebble Orientation in Fluvial Sediments", *J. Sediment. Petrol.,* in press.

SMITH, N. D., (1970), "The Braided Stream Depositional Environment: Comparison of the Platte River wih some Silurian Clastic Rocks, North-Central Appalachians", *Bull. Geol. Soc. Am.,* 81:2993-3014.

VAN STRAATEN, L. M. J. U., (1953), "Rhythmic Patterns in Dutch North Sea Beaches", *Geol. Mijnbouw,* 15:31-43.

WILLIAMS, P. F., and RUST, B. R., (1969), "The Sedimentology of a Braided River", *J. Sediment. Petrol.,* 39:649-679.

WOLMAN, M. G., (1954), "A Method of Sampling Coarse River-bed Material", *Trans. Am. Geophys. Union,* 35:951-956.

WOLMAN, M. G., and BRUSH, L.M., (1961), "Factors Affecting the Size and Shape of Stream Channels in Coarse Noncohesive Sands", *U.S. Geol. Surv., Prof. Pap.,* 282-G:183-210.

An Experimental Study of the Formation of Transverse Ribs: A Bed Form in Shallow Streams Carrying Coarse Alluvium

B. C. McDONALD,
Geological Survey of Canada

Transverse ribs constitute a distinctive bed form occupying the riffle portion of shallow streams with coarse alluvial beds. Ribs occur in a series of regularly spaced pebble, cobble, or boulder ridges extending across the channel and oriented transversely to current direction. They are widespread on braided alluvial plains and in high-gradient single-channel streams where they result in a stair-step arrangement forcing water to flow through a series of regularly spaced cascades.

Transverse ribs have been formed experimentally with pebbles in a laboratory flume. The pebbles are transported by supercritical flow and accumulate in a transition zone containing a hydraulic jump where the flow reverts to subcritical. Water waves in the transition zone are deformed by pebbles accumulating under them, until the waves collapse in an upstream direction and re-stabilize at a discrete distance upstream. Rib spacing is a function of slope and Froude Number upstream from the jump. Individual ribs form in seconds and are subsequently "fossilized" in a subcritical flow field as the hydraulic jump steps upstream.

It is possible that such supercritical flow events, with the additional bed roughness that transverse ribs represent, exert a strong influence on transportation of gravel and on channel morphology. Transverse ribs may also be useful to geologists as an indication of paleoflow conditions.